From AN OPEN LETTER TO THE PRESIDENT

It's a strain to come up with quips every day. . . . I must admit you had a few beauts on inaugural night. The only one I didn't understand was the joke about Guy Lombardo. You said at the Smithsonian that you and Pat had danced to Guy's orchestra on V-J night, and you hoped Guy Lombardo would still be playing when the next war ended.

I started to laugh at that one, and then I got pretty shaken. Mr. President, do you know something we don't know?

Sincerely,
A. B.

P.S.   How could Guy Lombardo still be playing after the next war?

Other Fawcett Crest Books
by *ART BUCHWALD*:

HAVE I EVER LIED TO YOU?

SON OF THE GREAT SOCIETY

AND THEN I TOLD THE PRESIDENT

ART BUCHWALD

The Establishment Is Alive and Well in Washington

A FAWCETT CREST BOOK

Fawcett Publications, Inc., Greenwich, Conn.

THE ESTABLISHMENT IS ALIVE AND WELL IN
WASHINGTON

A Fawcett Crest Book reprinted by arrangement with
G. P. Putnam's Sons

Library of Congress Catalog Card Number: 71-81648

"Confidential Note to the Reader" originally appeared in *Playboy*
magazine under the title "Why I Can't Write a Dirty Book,"
April 1969.

Published by Fawcett World Library
67 West 44th Street, New York, N.Y. 10036
Printed in the United States of America
October 1970

Contents

III. THE NOTE ON THE WHITE HOUSE DOOR

IV. GOD BLESS YOU, MRS. ROBINSON

V. WHO'S ON FIRST?

VI. THE COMPUTER THAT FAILED

VII. UP AGAINST THE WALL

VIII. HAVE GUN, WILL TRAVEL

IX. EYEBALL TO EYEBALL

X. THE KREMLIN WATCHERS

XI. THE CAPTURED DOCUMENT BUSINESS

XII. IS THE FOUR-LETTER WORD OBSOLETE?

The Establishment
Is Alive and Well
in Washington

CONFIDENTIAL NOTE TO THE READER

It is absolutely essential that anyone today who claims to be a writer must produce a pornographic book. It is a status symbol comparable with that of the Hemingway era, when in order to be a writer, you had to bag a lion.

You would think writing a pornographic book would be one of the easiest things in the world. Well, it isn't. I know, because I've been trying to write one for two years.

I think one of my problems is that I've been doing too much research. I like to be well versed in any subject I attack, so I spend hours upon hours reading other pornographic books, and by the time I get my reading done, I'm so excited I can't write myself.

Another thing that seems to have me stymied is that I don't know what kind of pornography to specialize in. I'm not sure whether I want to appeal to the flagellation-sadomasochistic school of writing, which has a limited but devoted audience:

"You're not going to whip me with that?" she cried hopefully.
"That's not all I'm going to do with you, you bitch," he chortled.

Or go commercial and write a wife-swapping novel:

"I've never done it with anyone but Fred," she cried, as she took off her slip.
"I've never done it with anyone but Sue," he said nervously, as he hung his pants on a chair.
She gasped as she gazed at his power, and suddenly Fred was the farthest thing from her mind.

But then I say to myself, "Everyone is writing wife-swapping books these days, and I'm not going to sell out for a Book-of-the-Month Club selection, no matter how much money there is in it."

So the thought occurs that maybe I should write a story of a woman who, because of a gang rape or some other beastly act, turns to another woman or women for consolation and love:

She sat in the chair, her skirt raised above her thighs, and looked into my face. My heart leaped as I saw her wet lips open and heard her voice say, "You know why I'm here." I fought back the impulse to drop to my knees and kiss those long beautiful white legs, but suddenly she rose from her chair, took my hand, and placed it on her breast. The room started spinning . . .

I guess there's a need for this type of book and I should be fulfilling it, but I've always believed that if you're going to write a novel, it should have social significance. And I keep thinking I could strike a blow for civil liberties if I could just find some way of dealing with a racial situation in a pornographic way:

She stared at the ebony face of her giant chauffeur and snarled, "Don't ever put your nigger hands on me, or my husband will kill you." The chauffeur tried to back out of the room in fear, but she blocked his way. Her negligee fell open and her snow-white breasts popped out. "Rape me," she cried, as she tore at his shirt. "Hurry, hurry, hurry."

I keep saying to myself, "If I do write a book like that, will I change anybody's mind about race relations, or will it just be another hopeless exercise in the white man patronizing the black?"

Besides, perhaps it is more important to write about big business and expose the brutal methods used to achieve power and wealth:

"Mrs. McCarthy, you realize, of course, that if you don't take off your clothes, your husband will lose his job and I will see that he never works in the advertising business again."

"But, Mr. Ryerson," she pleaded, knowing it was futile,

"don't make me do this. There must be some other way of saving George for losing the Soft-As-Sheep Carpet account."

Ryerson laughed; his beady eyes glinted. Then he got up from behind his desk and walked over to her. "Do you want to start unbuttoning your blouse, or do you want me to call Personnel?"

"No," she said, as she unzipped her skirt, trembling. "I have to do it for George."

As you can see, there are so many directions to go in these days when you want to write a pornographic book that it's almost impossible to stick with one theme. I imagine I could combine the themes, as many writers do, but the question I then have to ask myself is, "Is it literature?"

I keep struggling with the problem every day, and the more pornographic books I read, the more I realize how inadequate I am to write something that will last.

At the same time, I know that if I ever hope to be taken seriously as a writer, I must get down to work on my book. But my problem is that every time I start a paragraph:

Harry looked at the two girls in his bed and shook his head. How could he ever satisfy both of them and still make the seven ten for Scarsdale?

I say to myself, "Is this something the Supreme Court would want to read?"

1

You Can't Buck The
Establishment

UPPING PRISON REQUIREMENTS

I know you're not going to believe this, but Governor Lester Maddox of Georgia told a news conference recently, in answer to criticism about Georgia prison reform: "We're doing the best we can, and before we do much better, we're going to have to get a better grade of prisoner."

Once again, Governor Maddox hit the ax handle on the head. While penologists, sociologists, parole officers, and prison commissions all have been at odds about how to rehabilitate prisoners, Maddox has come up with the simplest and, without doubt, most sensible solution.

It has been known for years that prisons have been accepting a very low-class type of inmate, some without any education, others who are unstable, and some who are just plain antisocial.

No effort has been made to attract a better grade of prisoner, who would not only improve the caliber of our rehabilitation programs, but would also make society treat prisoners with the respect they deserve. For too long now we've been taking our prisoners for granted, and the standard for convicted felons has declined to a point where almost anyone can get into prison without his qualifications being questioned.

This trend must be reversed if we ever hope to rehabilitate our prisoners. The first thing to do would be to set up a recruiting drive in high schools and colleges to get a better class of inmate. This would have to be coupled with higher pay for prisoners, so being behind bars would become worthwhile.

Intelligence tests have to be set up at prisons to weed out those unfit to be imprisoned. Then personal interviews would be given to the prospective convicts to see if they've got what it takes to be rehabilitated. If they can't cut the mustard, then the prison should have the right to reject them.

17

Besides the tests and the interviews, the admissions board would demand references from the candidates to see that the convicted were of high moral character. It's also possible, in the case of federal prisons, that each Congressman and Senator could recommend two candidates for each penitentiary, as they do to West Point and Annapolis. In the case of state prisons, the governor could select the ones he believed had the most on the ball.

After making the application, taking his tests, submitting to a personal interview, and writing a composition telling why he believes he would make a good prisoner, the candidate would be sent home and told he would be notified by the FBI about whether he made it or not. If he failed to get in, the candidate could reapply again—after he robbed another bank.

Many people say that by being selective, we would be making too many demands on our prisoners; but the taxpayers are paying for them, and we should have the right to have the best convicts that money can buy.

I'm sure that Governor Maddox will be ridiculed for his ideas on prison reform, but he is the first person to come along and point out what is wrong with the penal system in this country. It isn't the courts, nor is it the physical facilities holding us back, but the fact that we have not concentrated on improving the quality of the people we take in.

Anyone who has ever visited a prison in this country knows that Governor Maddox is right. For years we have been scraping the bottom of the barrel for inmates, and it's no wonder they don't live up to our expectations.

It is only by raising the requirements for admission and paying a decent wage that we're going to get the grade of prisoner that Governor Maddox and the rest of us can be proud of.

WHAT TO DO AFTER WORLD WAR III

Anyone who doubts that the federal government is prepared for World War III just doesn't know how organized Washington really is. A short time ago someone who works for the Treasury Department received his instructions in writing on what he has to do in case of enemy attack.

They read as follows, and I haven't made a word of it up:

> . . . all National Office Employes with or without emergency assignments should follow this procedure. If you are prevented from going to your regular place of work because of an enemy attack—keep this instruction in mind—GO TO THE NEAREST POST OFFICE, ASK THE POSTMASTER FOR A FEDERAL EMPLOYE REGISTRATION CARD (sample shown on reverse side), FILL IT OUT AND RETURN IT TO HIM. He will see that it is forwarded to the office of the Civil Service Commission which will maintain the registration file for your area. When the Civil Service Commission receives your card, we will be notified. We can then decide where and when you should report for work. . . . You should obtain and complete your registration card as soon after enemy attack as possible, but not until you are reasonably sure where you will be staying for a few days. . . .

Nobody believes it will ever happen, but let us suppose that Robert Smiley (a fictitious person working for the Treasury Department) has just crawled out of the rubble after an enemy attack and remembers the instructions concerning civil defense for federal employees.

After walking for four days and 350 miles, Smiley finally finds a post office that is still standing. He staggers up to a window, but just as he gets there, the man behind it says, "Sorry, this window is closed," and slams it down.

Smiley stumbles to the next window and is told to get in line behind twenty other people. Two hours later he gets to the head of the line and croaks, "I want to register—"

"I'm sorry," says the post office clerk. "This window is just for stamps. Registered mail is at the next window."

"No, no," says Smiley. "I want a federal employee registration card."

"We don't sell those. Now do you want any stamps or don't you?"

"You see," says Smiley, holding onto the window, "I was instructed after the enemy attacked to find the nearest post office and fill out a card."

"You'd better try the parcel post window," the clerk suggests.

Smiley goes over to the parcel post window and gets in line with thirty people. Four hours later he is informed that the post office has run out of federal employee registration cards. They suggest he try another post office.

Smiley staggers out into the road and starts walking again. Four hundred miles up the highway he finds another post office. After catching his breath, he takes the card shakingly to the counter and starts to fill it out. But the pen won't work. He informs the postmaster of this, and the postmaster replies, "We know it, but there's nothing we can do about it. There's a war on."

"But I've got to register," says Smiley, "or the Civil Service Commission won't know where I am in case the United States Treasury wants to start up again. Couldn't I borrow your pen?"

"What? And ruin the point? Listen, why don't you go over to the Smithtown post office. I hear their pens are still in working order."

Clutching the card, Smiley walks 60 miles to Smithtown, where he fills it out. He mails it that very day.

Years later, Smiley is still waiting for a reply. For in his haste and fatigue, Smiley had forgotten to write down his return ZIP code.

VISITING A TAX SHELTER

You hear so much about tax shelters that I thought it was about time I went out and looked one over. I heard there was a beautiful one a few miles outside Houston, Texas, so, on a recent trip, I decided to make a detour and visit it.

It was on the property of a man named Ralston Loophole. When I arrived at his ranch, I was surprised to find nothing but a rickety old farmhouse. I rang the bell, and a grizzled old cowhand answered the door.

"I'm looking for Mr. Ralston Loophole," I said.

"He's out back yonder in his tax shelter," the cowhand said. "But you'd better be careful—he's got the place mined."

"Could you call him on the phone and tell him I'd like

to see him? Say I'm doing a piece on the most beautiful tax shelters in America for *Better Homes and Gardens*."

The cowhand came back in a few minutes. "OK, he'll see you. Mr. Loophole has to be careful. There's a lot of tax reform nuts hanging around lately."

He led me to the tax shelter, which was hidden among shrubbery, with only the door aboveground. The door was unlocked, and I climbed down. It was the most fantastic room I had ever been in. There were solid gold tables, crystal chandeliers, Gobelin tapestries on the wall, and a marble floor with a design in the center of a large loophole, which I assume was the family crest.

Mr. Loophole put out his hand. "Glad to meet ya," he said. "There's been a lot of criticism of tax shelters lately, and if I can do anything to change it, I'll be mighty happy to."

"Thank you, sir. This is a beautiful tax shelter," I said as he handed me a glass of champagne.

"It's right pretty, but it's just one of many I got."

"You mean you have more than one tax shelter?"

"Of course, boy. This is my oil-depletion tax shelter. I keep all my money here that I make from oil. The government can never find this place. Say, you aren't from the Feds, are you?"

"No, sir," I said. "Someday I hope to have a tax shelter of my own."

"Good for you, son. You've spoken like a true American. You know, there's lots of people in this country who are trying to do away with these oil-depletion tax shelters. They say we're not paying our full share of taxes. Well, let me tell you this. When we take oil out of the ground, there's no way of replacing it. That oil's gone forever. And if we have to pay full taxes, they'd be hurting the oil—not us.

"They want to take our oil shelters away from us, but, son, we aren't going to let them do it. Our sweat and our blood went into building these shelters."

"I'll be praying it never happens," I said as I put some caviar on toast. "What other tax shelters do you have?"

"I have one for cattle over in Oklahoma. Cattle depreciate—don't let anyone tell you otherwise. They get old, and they get tired, and if we had to pay taxes on them, those cattle would be miserable."

"No one should have to pay taxes on cattle," I said, helping myself to *foie gras*.

"Up in Chicago I have my real estate tax shelter. A man has to get a return on real estate, and that's what I keep the shelter there for. I also buy freight cars and airplanes, and I lease them back to the people I bought them from. That helps pay for the upkeep of the Chicago shelter. I forgot to mention my foundation in California. That's a beautiful shelter."

"How much money did you make last year with all these things?"

"Somewhere in the neighborhood of one hundred million dollars."

"How much federal tax did you pay?"

"Eight hundred dollars. But I can't figure how it happened. I thought I had all the loopholes covered."

THE MAN WHO PAID ALL HIS TAXES

When Emil Harwood Booster paid his taxes for the year, he discovered that he still had $117.50 left over in his bank account. It probably would have been overlooked; but he made the mistake of bragging to a friend in a bar about it, and he was overheard by an Internal Revenue Service agent, who reported it to his chief.

An emergency meeting was called of federal, state, county, and city tax officials to discover why Booster still had money left in the bank.

The IRS man said Booster's federal tax return had been checked, and it was all in order, so he couldn't be tried for any criminal violations. The state tax official said as far as his people could find out, Booster had paid all state taxes. The county man said his records showed that Booster was clean, and the city man said the same thing.

"Then," the IRS man said, "we can only come to one conclusion. If Booster still has money left over after he has paid his taxes, there is a loophole somewhere in the tax law."

"Wait a minute," said the county tax collector. "If anyone should get the one hundred seventeen dollars and fifty cents, it's the county. It would be very easy for us to raise Booster's real estate taxes."

"I object," said the city's representative. "It seems to me that the reason Booster got away with this is that our sales tax has been too low. We can up the sales tax by one percent, make it rctroactive, and inform Booster he owes us the one hundred seventeen dollars and fifty cents."

There was a lot of angry shouting, and finally the IRS man called the meeting to order. "Hold it. Shouting will do us no good. Let's look at this thing calmly. The way I see it, we are not as concerned about the one hundred seventeen dollars and fifty cents as we are about the fact that Booster still had money left over after he paid his taxes. Now we'll all have to admit that this is a very bad precedent, and if Booster can get away with it, everyone else will try to get away with it. We must discover what went wrong and see that it doesn't happen again."

"I'll tell you where it went wrong," the state man said. "We thought the President was going to put a surcharge of ten percent on everyone's income tax, so we didn't tax Booster the way we originally planned to."

"And," said the county man, "we thought the state was going to raise Booster's gasoline taxes, so we didn't raise his water and sewer taxes."

The city man said, "And we thought the county was going to put on a liquor and cigarette tax, so we thought we would pass up an entertainment tax until next year."

The IRS man said, "It seems to be a comedy of errors, and the only one who is laughing right now is Booster. The solution to the problem, as I see it, is to set up a coordinating committee and next year tax Booster an extra one hundred seventeen dollars and fifty cents, which he failed to pay this year. We could split the one hundred seventeen dollars and fifty cents among all of us, so Booster would have no idea what we were doing."

"It's not a bad idea," the state man said. "But I think there should be some punitive damages added. It's true that Booster didn't violate any laws, but he knew as well as we did that if he had any money at the end of the year, it belonged to one of us."

"That's true," the county man said. "He should have come clean and told us he still had money left in the bank and then let us adjust our tax rates accordingly."

"I say give it to the grand jury," the city man said.

"Any guy who has any money left over after he pays his taxes has got to be guilty of something."

Everyone agreed, and the IRS man said, "It's guys like Booster who give inflation a bad name."

CONGLOMERATES ARE "IN"

Almost every day you pick up the newspaper, some company is merging with another company. The average person has no idea what is happening, but it could eventually affect everybody in the United States. What it boils down to is that if you merge an apple company with another apple company, you're violating the antitrust laws. But if you merge an apple company with a banana company, then you're building a conglomerate, and whether you know it or not, conglomerates are the "in" things to own.

This is how conglomerates work.

Let us say that Dalinsky's Drugstore in Georgetown decides to merge with Fischetti's Meat Market in Bethesda, Maryland. Since neither Dalinsky nor Fischetti can agree on whose name to use, they call the company the Great American Drug and Meat Company. They issue stock, and it is immediately sold out, because any company that has the words "great," "American," "drug," and "meat" in it must have potential. Now, with the stock from their company, they make a bid to take over the Aetna Curtain Company, offering Aetna stockholders one share of GADAM for every two shares of Aetna.

Once the deal is completed, they go to the bank and borrow $500,000 on the Aetna Curtain Company, to buy the Markay Life Insurance Company.

Then, using the money in the Markay Life Insurance Company, they make a bid on the Mary Smith Pie and Bakery Company, offering one and a half shares of Markay for one and two thirds shares of Mary Smith.

It turns out that Mary Smith Pie and Bakery has a $3,000,000 surplus cash flow, so Dalinsky and Fischetti use this cash flow to buy the Carey Winston Life Preserver Company, which in spite of its name specializes in the building of Nike missiles.

With government contracts from the Carey Winston Life Preserver Company, as collateral, GADAM buys the Washington Green Sox baseball team, which it merges with the Norfolk Warriors, a basketball team that loses money but can come in handy to write off the profits of a TV station that GADAM is bidding on in Winnipeg.

With these companies as a nucleus, Dalinsky and Fischetti decide to make more acquisitions, because, as Dalinsky tells a *Time* magazine reporter who is doing a cover story on him titled the "Boy Wonder of Georgetown," "If you stand still, you die."

The next step for GADAM is to go to the First Citizens Bank of Wesley Heights and borrow $20,000,000 against the stock. With the money Dalinsky and Fischetti buy the Second Citizens Bank of Culpepper and then use the stock to purchase the First Citizens Bank of Wesley Heights.

From there it is only a matter of time before GADAM starts a mutual fund, a fried chicken franchise company, a Puerto Rican rum plant, and a senior citizens apartment complex in Fairbanks, Alaska.

In less than three years Dalinsky, who put up $30, and Fischetti, who put up $25, control $3 billion worth of businesses and are each worth $50,000,000 on paper. The only danger is that if either Dalinsky's Drugstore or Fischetti's Meat Market lose the lease on its store, the whole conglomerate pyramid could fall down. When you get right down to it, that's the only part of their business that Dalinsky and Fischetti understand.

MONEY CRISIS QUIZ

Now that everyone understands the world monetary crisis, we're going to give you your final quiz:

1. If I have five French francs and you have three West German deutsche marks, what will we have all together?

ANSWER. One of the damnedest money messes since World War II.

2. If I want to sell my French francs for German marks at 10 percent less than they're officially quoted, what currency will be hurt the most?

A. The British pound.

3. Why?

A. Because it's tied to the American dollar.

4. When the American dollar gets in serious trouble, what country sells its dollars and demands gold, to make it go down further?

A. France.

5. When the French franc gets in trouble, what country agrees to go to its rescue and shore it up with its own gold?

A. The United States.

6. Why?

A. Because of the British pound.

7. When the British pound gets into trouble, who is the first person to demand that it be devalued?

A. President Charles de Gaulle.

8. When the French franc gets in trouble, who is the *last* person to agree to its devaluation?

A. President Charles de Gaulle.

9. Why?

A. Because of the West German mark.

10. What has the German mark got to do with the French franc?

A. The West German mark is undervalued because the Germans don't have enough inflation. The French franc is overvalued because the French have too much inflation.

11. What is the solution?

A. The British have to tighten their belts.

You have a coffee break now before we go on with the quiz. All right, let's continue:

12. What happens to all the gold that is supposed to support world currencies?

A. It's bought by the Swiss for people who have numbered accounts in Zurich.

13. When they buy the gold, what happens to the currencies?

A. Except for the Swiss franc and the German mark, they go down.

14. Why?

A. Because everyone is afraid of the British pound.

15. What can France do to restore confidence in the French franc?

A. Attack the American dollar.

16. How can they do this?

A. By using the money we've lent them to preserve their franc.

17. Why would we allow this?

A. To preserve the British pound.

18. Who will President de Gaulle blame if his reforms don't work?

A. The United States.

19. Who will get the credit if De Gaulle can pull it off?

A. That's a stupid question.

20. What can the average American do until the money crisis blows over?

A. Take an Englishman to lunch.

THEY WANT TO HELP US

The worst part of the economic dollar crisis is that everyone is telling the United States what to do about it. For twenty-five years we have been advising other countries how to shore up their economies, but now the tables are turned, and we have to sit and listen to them. De Gaulle started it, but even the smaller countries are getting into the act.

The U.S. Ambassador to Zemululu was recently called in by Zemululu's Minister of Finance. After shaking hands with him, the minister invited the ambassador to sit on the dirt floor of his tent near the fire.

"Mr. Ambassador," the minister said as he popped a betel nut into his mouth, "Zemululu is very concerned about your dollar crisis."

"It's good to hear you say that," the ambassador replied as he tried to keep a lizard from running up his leg.

"You see, we feel we have a stake in America's economy, and what affects you will affect us."

"Why do you say that?" the ambassador asked as he knocked a spider off his sleeve.

"Well, as you know, most of our aid comes from the United States, and we certainly don't want help from a country that is having trouble with its currency."

"Of course, you don't," said the ambassador. "We're grateful you've been playing along with us this long."

"Yes, but I must warn you since we are an underdeveloped country, we can't play along with you much longer. The Zemululu people demand that the country that helps them show more fiscal responsibility or they'll have to get their aid somewhere else."

"We're doing the best we can," the American ambassador said.

"From what I can read, this apparently is not good enough," the minister said. "It seems to me you're going to have to tighten your belts, straighten out your balance of payments, and win the respect of the worldwide banking community."

"But how?" the ambassador asked.

"Zemululu economists have just completed a study of the United States' economy. We feel that among the measures you must take to strengthen the dollar is to export more than you import, increase your gross national product, and raise taxes. Unless you are willing to do this, we will not be able to accept your financial assistance."

"But those are very strong measures."

"Mr. Ambassador, we can't help you if you're not willing to help yourselves. It is not just a question of economic stability. You are also lacking political stability, and you will never get anywhere if you don't win the hearts and minds of your own people."

"You mean you want us to change our political system, too?"

"Zemululu does not like to interfere in the affairs of another country, but to be frank with you, I cannot justify to my people accepting aid from a country whose domestic affairs are in such chaos."

"How much time do we have?" the American ambassador asked.

"Not much," the minister said. "We're planning to have a dam, and if your gold situation doesn't improve, we may ask the Russians to build it for us."

"I'll pass your thoughts on to Washington, but I hope you won't make up your mind until we have a chance to prove ourselves."

"Mr. Ambassador, the people of Zemululu have the greatest respect for America, and we are certainly aware of the problems of an overdeveloped country. At the same time, we feel if we don't get tough, you people will let things slide, and we'll be stuck with a bunch of aid dollars that have no value."

"Thank you for your kindness and help," the American ambassador said, killing a snake with his foot.

"It's perfectly all right." The minister smiled. "After all, if we were in trouble, you'd probably do the same for us."

YOU CAN'T BUCK THE ESTABLISHMENT

Woe to the person in this country who attacks the Establishment. It isn't jail or even physical harm that he must fear. His main problem is that by attacking the Establishment, he automatically becomes a member of it, and there is no greater punishment in the world.

Let us take the case of Samuel Suchard, a pro-Maoist, antiwar, antidraft Leninist-anarchist. Having led demonstrations against the White House, the Pentagon, the U.S. aircraft carrier *Enterprise*, and the YWCA, Suchard was finally caught by the Establishment and dragged down to the Metropolitan Club for lunch.

There he faced a table of smiling, friendly faces.

"Suchard," one of the Establishment members said, "We've had our eye on you for some time, and we think you have what it takes to be one of us."

"A pox on you," Suchard said. "I'm against the Establishment with its stinking rules and fancy clothes and bloated imbeciles. I despise you all." To make his point, Suchard threw his soup on the floor.

Instead of getting angry, the rest of the people at the table applauded.

"Of course, you do," said a second member of the party. "And you have every right to hate us. It's for this reason that we think you would make a marvelous member of the power structure. How would you like a grant from the Ford Foundation, so when you attack the Establishment, you won't have to worry about financial problems?"

"To hell with a grant from the Ford Foundation, man. I'm not selling out for any lousy grant. I'm a revolutionist."

Suchard picked up his steak and started to eat it with his fingers.

A third member at the table spoke up. "You don't have to take the Ford grant if you don't want to. Would you consider a lecture tour under our sponsorship? You could go around the country speaking before Rotary and Kiwanis luncheons explaining why you're disenchanted with society and what we have done wrong. There's a big demand for such speakers now."

For the first time Suchard started losing some of his cool. "What are you guys trying to do to me? Don't you understand? I'm against every American institution from the flag to the space program. I want to tear the very fabric of this society apart."

"Of course, you do, Suchard, and we respect you for it. The Establishment is always open to criticism in spite of things you hear to the contrary. We could even arrange for you to be on *Meet the Press*, where you could voice your discontent to millions and millions of people at one time. Or, if you prefer, we could give you your own television show, where you could discuss your own opinions in the manner of David Susskind."

Suchard wiped his mouth with his sleeve. "I—I—I—you guys are trying to trap me. I want to get out of here."

The man sitting next to Suchard put his hand gently on Suchard's arm and said almost in a whisper, "Sam, how would you like to be on the cover of *Time* magazine, as spokesman for all alienated youth?"

Suchard looked from face to face. "I couldn't do it. I mean, what would the guys say?"

"We'd even throw in the cover of *Newsweek*, Sam."

Suchard said dreamily, "The covers of *Time* and *Newsweek*."

"It wouldn't just end there, Sam. We could get you appointed to a government commission to study violence among our youth. We could make you a director of a poverty program; you could meet with the President at the White House, lunch with David Rockefeller, get an honorary degree from Harvard, become a member of the Burning Tree Golf Club, and the beauty of it is, you wouldn't have to give up one of your ideals."

"All right, already," cried Suchard. "I'll do anything you ask. Just leave me alone."

"We knew you'd see it our way, Sam. Would you like to come down to the racquet club with us after lunch for a few sets of squash?"

2

Little Old Lady
In Tennis Shoes

IN PRAISE OF LYNDON JOHNSON

When Lyndon Baines Johnson was preparing to leave office was the first time in the five years since he became President that you couldn't hear an unkind word about him. His most ardent critics had changed their tunes, and it's hard to believe that they were talking about the same man they had discussed the year before.

One of his toughest critics was heard to say at a party, "He may have made mistakes, but you can't fault him on what he tried to do."

Another Johnson nonadmirer agreed, "If Nixon does half as well as Lyndon did, he'll be a good President."

"Nixon won't. They don't make Presidents like LBJ anymore."

"You know what I liked about Johnson?" another former anti-Johnson man said. "His style. He had a free-wheeling style which made you admire him. I think Nixon's biggest weakness is he has no style."

"You can say that again. Lyndon came from Texas, and at least you knew where he stood on the issues."

"You're right. You have no idea where Nixon stands on anything."

"Johnson really worked as President," said another man, who used to get red when Lyndon's name was mentioned. "Maybe he had his faults, but he also had his strengths, and his strengths outnumbered his faults."

"Nixon's faults outnumber his strengths."

A lady nodded her head. "I can't stand Nixon on TV. At least when you saw Johnson on TV, you knew he was sincere."

The lady next to her agreed. "President Johnson had kind eyes and a sincere chin."

"He was good to the poor," I said, not wanting to look as if I had anything against Johnson.

"And he worried about the black people," a former McCarthy supporter said.

"Nixon won't hold a candle to him when it comes to what Johnson did for education."

"And don't forget the redwood trees in California," someone else said. "To this day, people don't know how Johnson saved the redwood trees."

"I think when I remember Johnson," said another person, "it will be for Medicare."

"You know Nixon won't do anything for sick people."

"Why should he? They aren't his people."

I tried to bring some balance back into the conversation.

"I guess if you'd have to fault Johnson at all, it would be in foreign affairs."

Everyone turned on me angrily.

"He thought he was doing the right thing at the time."

"He was only following out the policies of Kennedy and Eisenhower."

"Do you think Nixon is going to do any better?"

I tried to recoup. "There'll never be another Lady Bird."

Another ex-Johnson hater said, "I'm going to miss the whole Johnson family, including Jack Valenti's daughter."

"Tricia will never be another Lynda Bird."

"And Julia will never be another Luci."

I was starting to choke up. "I don't want him to go," I cried.

"None of us do," a former ADA president sobbed.

"The worst part is that he'll never know how we felt about him."

"Yeah, and Nixon won't even have the class to tell him."

PRESIDENT OF THE WORLD

Everywhere I went in Europe the summer before the 1968 Presidential elections they asked the same question: "Who's going to be the next President of the United States?" Americans don't realize it, but Europeans feel they have as much stake in the outcome of our Presidential elections as we do, and the results are watched with as much trepidation in Rome, Italy, as they are in Rome, New York.

This worldwide concern over the choice of United

States Presidents has reached such enormous proportions that I believe there is only one solution to the problem, and that is it's time America opened up the Presidential elections to *everyone*.

Any citizen of any country, who is over twenty-one years of age, should be permitted to vote for the President of the United States. In this way the next President would be chosen on the basis of his popularity throughout the world, instead of just the fifty states.

The advantages of holding such an election would far outweigh the costs of installing voting booths in such far-off places as Sierra Leone and Borneo. For one thing, if the President of the United States were elected globally, he would have a world-wide mandate from the people, and no one could complain that the President of the United States was just representing the interests of his own country.

Since everyone would have a say about the next U.S. President, the people of other nations would be obligated to support him and back him in the great decisions that affect them. It is my belief that if we open up the elections to everyone on the globe, the attacks on the dollar will cease, the demonstrations against American Embassies will come to a halt, and the U.S. Sixth Fleet will be welcome in every port in the world.

I know there are nit pickers who will say the idea is impracticable. They'll point out that it will be very costly for Presidential candidates to campaign in every part of the world, and there is always the language barrier that has to be considered when you open American elections to outside countries.

But this is not a serious objection. For four years now Richard Nixon has been traveling all over the world running for President of the United States, and it hasn't hurt him. With satellite television, the other candidates could get over their message with subtitles. There would be no difficulty for an American political campaign to be adapted to a global affair.

The critics will say that people in many parts of the world are not sufficiently informed to vote for an American President, but this, of course, is a canard.

Everyone knows about American politics and even in the Soviet Union, where I just came from, the Russians who refused to express opinions about their own government expressed strong opinions about ours.

The only way we can get the rest of the world to support the United States is to permit them to choose our President. Why should Americans take the responsibility for electing Nixon, Rockefeller, Reagan, Humphrey, or McCarthy when everyone else is going to criticize our choice anyway?

LITTLE OLD LADY IN TENNIS SHOES

No one heard from the Little Old Lady in Tennis Shoes during the 1968 election year, although in 1964 she was Barry Goldwater's staunchest supporter and was quoted constantly during the entire campaign.

I was fortunate to run into her one day on the street shortly before the Republican Convention. Except for the fact that she looked a little grayer and her shoes were a little more scuffed, she had changed little during Lyndon Johnson's years in office.

"Hello, Little Old Lady in Tennis Shoes," I said. "It's good to see you again."

"You say that every four years, but you never come to see me when there aren't any elections going on."

"I'm sorry," I apologized, "but I've been awfully busy covering President Johnson."

"I'll bet you have," she cackled. "You all laughed at me in 1964, but in your heart you know I was right."

"Tell me, Little Old Lady in Tennis Shoes, what have you been doing for the past four years?"

"Perfecting my serve. When my man lost, I went back to tennis. I've never played better. You got time for a couple of sets? I've got my racket in my shopping bag here."

"Thank you, but I really don't have time to play now."

"Too bad. I could whip the pants off you."

"I know this is a personal question, but who are all the little old ladies in tennis shoes supporting this year?"

"Well, that Ronald Reagan seems like such a nice young man. He's no Barry Goldwater when it comes to thinking; but he dresses so neatly, and he's got such a sincere quality in his voice. I even liked him before he went into politics."

"You had to like him then," I said.

"Reagan stands for God, home, and country," she said, swinging her tennis racket for emphasis. "He believes in the American virtues that all of us hold dear."

"How do you feel about Rockefeller?"

"That Socialist? Do you know he tried to steal the nomination away from Barry Goldwater in 1964? He would have, if we hadn't booed him at the convention."

"Was that you tennis ladies booing Rockefeller?"

"Well, it wasn't Happy," she chuckled as she hit a tennis ball across the street.

"How do you feel about Nixon?"

She paused in the middle of a swing. "Old Tricky Dicky. We tennis shoe people liked the old Nixon. The new Nixon gets on your nerves. If we have to go that route we will, but it's the last time."

"You wouldn't consider supporting a Democrat, would you?"

"You must be kidding," she said. "I wouldn't even play one doubles."

"It's that bad, huh?"

"Look, Sonny, we little old ladies in tennis shoes have very high standards. We're not going to throw our vote away on leftist, pinko, deficit spenders who want to fluoridate our drinking water. You sure you don't have time for one set?"

"I wish I did," I said regretfully, "but I have to get back to the office."

She put her tennis racket back in her shopping bag. "Too bad," she said. "I've really perfected my backhand."

"I guess I'll see you at the Republican convention."

"You bet your sweet life you will, Sonny," she said, jumping over an imaginary net to shake my hand. "And this time we're going to give it to Rockefeller good. Those Eastern Establishment Socialists just never learn."

FAREWELL TO POVERTY

My friend McAlister, the only poor person I know who will admit it, was very depressed the other day.

"I knew they'd get tired of us very fast."

"What do you mean, McAlister?" I asked him.

"Poverty is out. You don't hear people talking about it anymore. This year's big thing in Congress is hunger."

"Well, you have to be realistic about this, McAlister. Congress can't be expected to stay with one problem very long. They've already had their hearings on poverty. They have to go on to something else, or the American people will lose interest."

"I guess you're right," said McAlister. "Don't get me wrong. I don't have anything against hunger. Some of my best friends are hungry. But I was hoping that they would at least solve the poverty problems before they went on to hunger."

"Your mistake, McAlister, if you don't mind my saying so, is that you don't understand the attention span of the American people. They can't stay with any subject too long. They gave poverty a fair shake. That's all we heard about for two years. That's plenty long enough. If you can't solve poverty in the United States in two years, then it's obviously unsolvable. Besides, it's not much fun to be reminded all the time that the United States has a poor-people problem."

McAlister sighed. "I understand all that, and I was under no illusion that anyone could solve my problems. But it was all the attention I got that I miss. Do you know I was interviewd by four different foundations in one week? Reporters used to buy me drinks in exchange for my telling them what it was like to be poor. There were TV cameras all over the neighborhood. College kids from Vassar and Swarthmore moved in during the summer to pull us up by our bootstraps. It might not have done much good, but the excitement sure relieved the tedium of being poor."

"OK, McAlister. You people had your day. But we can't stay with poverty forever. It doesn't have any sex appeal. The more you talk about it, the madder people get. And if you try to do anything about it, then you're really stepping on people's toes. Now hunger is a different kettle of fish. All you have to do with hunger is give people food."

"Why didn't they do it in the past if it was that simple?"

"Because Congress didn't know you could make hunger

a political issue until this year. You've got to think of them, too."

"There I go," said McAlister, "only thinking of myself."

I started to feel sorry for him. "McAlister, don't get discouraged. Poverty may make a comeback. Perhaps it won't be called poverty, but they'll call it something else."

"Maybe they could call it pro football," McAlister said. "Americans don't seem to lose interest in that."

"Let's not lose our perspective," I said angrily. "Pro football is not a joking matter."

THE LITTLE OLD PHRASEMAKER

The largest manufacturer of political rhetoric in the United States is Hiram Thesaurus, with whom I was fortunate to talk at the 1968 Republican National Convention in Miami Beach.

Thesaurus was standing in front of one of his retail stands taking inventory, when I asked him, "How's business?"

"Great," he said. "All the rhetoric makers expect 1968 to be the biggest year we've ever had. We got off to a good start at the Republican Convention, and there is no reason why we shouldn't do as well or better in Chicago."

"What item has been moving best?"

" 'Law and order' has been the biggest seller this year. We can't even keep the law and order rhetoric in stock. The minute it's put out on the counter, it's grabbed up."

"What else is selling?"

" 'Peace at home and abroad' is a very big item. I don't think there's a politician running for office this year who hasn't bought at least one. 'The crisis of the cities' is also moving very well, but the one that really surprised us was 'a piece of the action.' We made a few as samples, and before we knew it, everyone was using it to describe what the minorities wanted. I sold one to Barry Goldwater, one to Senator Brooke, and Nixon bought a gross from me wholesale. We've had so many orders on this one that a lot of politicians have to wait two weeks for delivery on it."

"How's the 'cry for new leadership' going?"

"That's been a smash down here, of course, but we were

prepared for it. I'm not too sure how well it will do in Chicago, though we have had advance orders on it from the McCarthy people."

"In the manufacture of political rhetoric, do you design your own phrases or do you just copy what's been used before?"

"Both. We have the standard rhetoric items such as 'fiscal responsibility' and 'politics of expediency' which the politicians use every four years. But we also have to come up with new rhetoric which will catch the ear of the voter."

"Such as?"

"Well, as you remember, in 1964 a lot of political rhetoric was aimed against the press. This year we've designed rhetoric which will attack the Supreme Court. You can't imagine what a demand there is this year for 'coddling the criminals.' Another one which we came up with is 'Let's not ask what is wrong with America, but what's right with America.' "

"I see you have one there on the counter titled 'Tell it like it is.' "

"That's been selling like mad, almost as well as 'a man for our time.' Another big surprise is our erosion kit. It comes in a set: 'erosion of the cities,' 'erosion of the dollar,' 'erosion of moral values,' and 'erosion of America's prestige abroad.' We've also been doing well with 'rebuilding the urban and slum areas' and 'facing up to the challenges and responsibilities of the disenfranchised.' "

As we were talking, a politician came up with his campaign manager and said, "Do you have any more 'new and dynamic leadership' rhetoric?"

"Yes, sir," Thesaurus said. "How are you fixed for 'excessive federal spending'?"

"Give me whatever you've got. Do you have any rhetoric on the *Pueblo?*"

"We're running a special on 'a fourth-rate military power humiliating the most powerful nation in the world.' "

"I'll take two."

"Right. Now what about 'one nation under God, indivisible, with liberty and justice for all'?"

"No," said the politician, "I don't want to lose the South in my campaign."

THE GLOATING REPUBLICAN

The first few weeks after the 1968 Presidential elections were very tough for those people who had rooted for Vice President Humphrey to win the election. After gloating at the Republicans for eight years, the Democrats finally got some of their own medicine back, and it wasn't easy for the Dems to accept the loss with good grace.

The only Democrat I know who has been able to handle it is my friend Rumpelmeyer. I bumped into him at lunch the other day and he said, "Sharkey's joining me in a few minutes, and he's going to be impossible over the Nixon win. He specifically invited me to lunch so I would eat crow."

"Why did you accept?"

"I thought I'd have some fun. Hang around and see what happens."

I took a seat, and a few minutes later Sharkey came in bubbling and bouncing, hardly able to contain himself.

"Well, Rump," he said after he had ordered a drink. "What did you think of the elections?"

"Who won?" Rumpelmeyer said. "I've been out of town for a week and haven't seen a paper."

Sharkey flushed. "Don't give me that, Rumpelmeyer. You know damn well who won."

"No, I really don't, Sharkey. The last I heard was that Agnew called the New York *Times* a fat Jap."

Sharkey waved his finger. "You're not going to trick me with that innocent routine, Rump. I've waited eight years for this moment."

Rumpelmeyer said, "Good heavens, Sharkey. You're not going to tell me Nixon won the election?"

Sharkey yelled, "You're darn tootin' he won, and you're eating your heart out."

Rumpelmeyer turned to me. "Is it true?"

"I'm afraid it is," I said. "Everyone's conceded it but Mayor Daley."

"Well," said Rumpelmeyer, "this calls for a celebration."

"I'll do the celebrating," Sharkey yelled. "I rooted for him. You didn't."

"I think that's rather selfish of you, Sharkey. After all,

Nixon is my President, too. I believe we should drink to him."

Sharkey was getting so mad he gripped the table. "Don't patronize me, Rump. I didn't come here to listen to you toast Nixon."

"But, Sharkey," Rumpelmeyer said, "I don't know why you should be so upset about my wanting to toast Nixon. After all, it's only a Presidential election, and if you've seen one President, you've seen them all."

"Yes, Rumpelmeyer," Sharkey said, gritting his teeth. "But the difference is that my man won and your man lost, and that means your people are out and my people are in."

"So it does," Rumpelmeyer said. "I'll drink to that."

"You won't drink to it!" Sharkey said. "I'll drink to it!"

"I don't know what's gotten into you, Sharkey. I'm sure Nixon's happier about all this than you are."

"What do you know about Nixon?" Sharkey cried. "I voted for him."

"Everyone knows about Nixon," Rumpelmeyer said. "He'll probably make a fine President."

I thought Sharkey was going to hit him. "Rump, we may not have agreed politically with each other in the past, and we may have had our differences on the future of this country, but I never thought you'd stoop so low as to steal my one moment of triumph, after I waited eight miserable, lonely years."

"You're right, Sharkey. This is your moment, so let me buy you a drink."

Sharkey rose from the table and screamed, "I'll buy my own drinks! Can't you get it through your head? *I won!*"

He wheeled around and walked out of the restaurant, leaving his coat behind.

Rumpelmeyer shrugged his shoulders and said to me, "The Nixon people are certainly taking their win awfully hard."

LOBBY SWAPPING IN D.C.

One of the groups most affected by the change from a Democratic Administration to a Republican one is the lobbyists of vested interests. After the 1968 elections, having wined and dined Democrats for the past eight years, the capital's lobbyists had to convince their clients that they were in as solid with the Nixon people as they had been with the Kennedy and Johnson appointees.

I happened to stop in to visit a lobbyist friend of mine to find out how he was doing.

He was talking on the phone as I was ushered in. "Don't worry about a thing, Mr. Blathering. As luck would have it my sister went to school with Pat Nixon ... No, they weren't in the same class but they used to pass each other in the hall all the time ... What do you mean I told you five years ago my sister went to school with Lady Bird Johnson? ... I did? ... Oh, yeah, that was my other sister ... You see, I have two sisters ... Mr. Blathering, I assure you there isn't a member of the Nixon administration that I couldn't get on the phone right now ... Yes, sir, I'll call you back."

My friend saw me standing there. "Sit down a minute." He then called his secretary. "Did Bob Finch call back yet?"

"No, sir. I've called him twelve times."

My friend said, "Keep calling."

"What's with the Finch?" I asked.

"It's a long story. In 1966 I got a letter from Finch asking me to contribute to his campaign for lieutenant governor of California. I threw the letter in the wastepaper basket."

"That was a stupid thing to do," I said.

"Well, how the hell was I to know that someday he'd be Secretary of Health, Education, and Welfare?"

"What good is talking to him now?"

"I'm going to explain to him the letter got lost, and I don't want him to think I forgot."

"Do you believe he'll buy that?"

"I guess not," he said, discouraged. "But I have to think of something to convince my clients I've got influence with the Nixon administration. If you could only get invited to one of those Billy Graham prayer sessions at the White House."

"They're not open to the public," I said.

"It really doesn't seem fair," he said. "You work with people for eight years, you get to know their wives and their kids, you build up close personal relationships, and then, zap, they go and change administrations, and you have to start all over again with a whole new set of friends."

"I guess you can't stay friends with people after they're out of the government," I said.

"You can, but why would you want to?"

"You have a point," I agreed. "Where do you think your biggest problem is going to be?"

"Probably in defense. David Packard is Undersecretary of Defense and my problem is, what can a lobbyist do for a man who has three hundred million dollars?"

The secretary came back in. "It's Mr. Blathering again. He wants to know if you met anybody yet."

My friend was perspiring. "Hi there, Mr. Blathering . . . No, I haven't heard from Bob Finch, but I think I have a breakthrough. It turns out my kid and Secretary of Defense Mel Laird's fourteen-year-old kid are on the same baseball team at Landon . . . How do you like that for coincidence? . . . Please don't be so nervous, Mr. Blathering . . . Of course, I'm aware of your problem . . . I'll take it up with the Attorney General on Monday."

He called Attorney General Mitchell's office and spoke to his secretary. "Hi, there, my name is Grumbottom, and my sister used to go to school with the Attorney General's wife. . . ."

KENNEDY AND THE ESKIMOS

Senator Teddy Kennedy has become a pariah as far as the Republicans are concerned, and anything he does from now until 1972 is being viewed with fear and suspicion.

The word is even out on him in Alaska.

Two Eskimos were fishing in a hole in the ice about 300 miles north of Nome when they saw a large crowd arriving at their village.

"I wonder what's going on over there," Nikko said.

"It's probably Senator Kennedy's Senate committee investigating the plight of the Eskimos in Alaska," Tula replied.

"Let's stay away from that," Nikko said. "If we have our picture taken with Kennedy, we'll have every Republican in Congress on our backs."

"I guess you're right, but I'd be curious to see Kennedy. He may not get up this way very soon again," Tula said.

"Please, Tula. You may want to run for village chief someday, and if you shake hands with Kennedy, the Republicans will bring it up in the campaign. Besides, we still don't have our dinner."

"I can't understand why the fish aren't biting today," Tula said. "Maybe the TV cameras are scaring them away."

"Hey, Tula, why don't we hold a press conference and say Senator Kennedy and his tour scared all our fish? That could get you launched in politics."

Tula became excited. "Nikko, you're a genius. I'd be on the Huntley-Brinkley and Cronkite shows. I might even make the cover of *Life* magazine. The Republicans would invite me to address their fund-raising dinners. They'd probably even have me over to the White House with Senator Dirksen."

"Culturally, it might ruin you to be taken out of your primitive habitat and be thrown into modern civilization, but it would still be better than eating fish every night."

"Not to mention getting away from these cold winters," Tula said.

Nikko said, "You could even run for governor of Alaska on the Republican ticket."

Tula said, "And maybe someday I could become Secretary of the Interior."

"Hey, look. Isn't that Arni presenting Senator Kennedy with a seal-tusk paperweight?"

"The fool. He's just destroyed his political career," Tula said. "Leave it to Arni to be in the wrong place at the wrong time."

"We'd better go over there and hold our press conference before the TV and newspaper people take off."

"Wait a minute. I think I've got a bite. Yes, I do have a bite. Look, Nikko, it's a big one."

"Throw it back," Nikko shouted. "You'll ruin the press conference."

"Are you crazy? This is my dinner."

"But what about your political career?"

"I'd rather have something to eat tonight, if it's all the same to you."

"Tula, as your campaign manager, I beg you to throw back that fish."

"Not me, Nikko. I'd rather eat than be President."

Nikko shook his head. "No wonder we Eskimos can't get out of our rut."

3

The Note On The
White House Door

NIXON'S FIRST FIVE AND ONE-HALF DAYS

When Richard Nixon had been President of the United States for five and a half days, I decided it was not too early for historians to judge what kind of President he had been. These were my observations:

So far the Nixon administration has failed to make any gains in the fight against crime. If anything, the crime rate has gone up since he has been in the White House, and when historians write about his first five and a half days, they will have to say that Mr. Nixon was unable to solve law and order, the number one problem in the country.

As far as the economy goes, President Nixon has not been able to bring about any great tax reforms during his first week in office. But here he cannot be solely to blame. A recalcitrant Democratic Congress has been sitting on its hands since Tuesday and has refused to take up any of Mr. Nixon's legislation.

The peace talks have been moving at a snail's pace in Paris, and many Americans are disappointed that they may go on another week. It was hoped that when Nixon moved into the White House, we'd have a peace treaty with the North Vietnamese by Friday.

Also, President Nixon's promise to improve relations with the Soviet Union has yet to bear fruit. Since he has been in office, the Russians have given no indication that they want to talk about mutual matters concerning our countries. Critics of the Nixon administration feel something should have been started by now, and the big question they are asking is: How much time does he need to get the ball rolling?

We are no nearer the moon today than we were when Mr. Nixon was sworn in on Monday.

This has many people concerned, because it was hoped that we would have an American on the moon as soon as a Republican President took office.

When historians write their books about President Nixon's first week in office, they will also point out that he was unable to resolve the Middle East crisis by Sunday. People close to President Nixon say this was one of his biggest disappointments, because he wanted to get that part of the world settled so he could go on to other things.

Other areas where the Nixon administration has failed are Latin America, Biafra, and San Francisco State. Defenders of the administration said that Mr. Nixon would turn his attention to these problems in his second week. But opponents of the Nixon policies say he's had already enough time to get them resolved.

On the plus side, Mr. Nixon's relations with the press have been excellent, and no President has been treated as well during his first five and a half days in office.

While his legislative record, so far, leaves much to be desired, when the history of these first five and a half days is written, no one will say that Mr. Nixon didn't try.

Mysterious, pragmatic, a loner, devoted to his family, a man who came back from the ashes of defeat, Richard Nixon will go down during his first week as a strong President seeking to heal the wounds of a nation wracked with fear and despair.

With only one thousand four hundred fifty-four and a half days to go in his term, the President can do little more now than tidy up the things he started in his first five and a half days.

The question people are now asking is whether Richard Nixon will run again or whether he is fed up with the job that has made so many demands on him. Those who know him well say that he believes he has a mission and, despite the disappointment of the first five and one-half days, he likes the job and is thriving on it.

"Perhaps," said an aide, "after a couple of weeks he may think otherwise. But I can assure you that if he had his first five and a half days to do all over again, Dick Nixon wouldn't have done anything differently."

OPEN LETTER TO THE PRESIDENT

DEAR PRESIDENT NIXON:

This will be the first of many letters I will write to you

in the next four years telling you how to run the country. You'll be very happy to hear that there is no charge for this advice since I feel it's my duty as a loyal American to help the President solve the many problems of the day.

Now the first thing, Mr. President, I think you're going to have to stop is the jokes. I watched you on television making the rounds of the inaugural balls and while I chuckled as much as you did at everything you had to say, my fear is that you can't keep up that high pace of humor and also perform the duties of President of the United States.

The trouble with being President and using witty lines is that by the third time you've told them, everyone in the country has heard them, and you get to sound like a recorded announcement.

I'm not saying you shouldn't have humor in your administration, because heaven knows the country needs a laugh, but I think you could turn this problem over to your Vice President, Mr. Agnew, or if worse comes to worst your Secretary of the Interior, Walter Hickel.

As a matter of fact, there are many people in Washington, including Congress, the Supreme Court and the Pentagon, who can provide the laughs for this country, without your having to work on your own humor.

It's a strain to come up with quips every day, and while there is no doubt in my mind that you could do it, I don't want you to feel you have to. Warren Harding and Calvin Coolidge did tremendous jobs as Presidents, and I doubt if you'll find six humorous things either one of them said that people are still quoting.

I must admit you had a few beauts on inaugural night. That one about Spiro Agnew marrying above himself was a rib tickler, and the one about someone giving you the key to the White House and you thought you'd better go there was good enough for *Laugh-In*.

The only one I didn't understand was the joke about Guy Lombardo. You said at the Smithsonian that you and Pat had danced to Guy Lombardo's orchestra on V-J night, and you hoped Guy Lombardo would still be playing when the next war ended.

I started to laugh at that one, and then I got pretty shaken. Mr. President, do you know something we don't know?

I know it's gratuitous for me to discuss your humor with you, but I thought if I mentioned it now, it might save you time later on. No one can come up with as many good one-liners as you did on inaugural night, and keep it up for four years.

I've talked it over with my colleagues, Russ Baker, Art Hoppe, Herblock, Bill Mauldin, Paul Conrad, and many other people in the political humor business, and we all agreed that you should be spared the problem of entertaining us while running the country. To paraphrase the Greyhound Bus advertisement: "Go Air Force One and leave the joking to us."

Sincerely,
A.B.

P.S. How could Guy Lombardo still be playing after the next war?

THE NOTE ON THE WHITE HOUSE DOOR

When President Richard Nixon and his wife, Pat, came back from the swearing-in ceremonies at the Capitol, they found a note from Mr. Johnson pinned on the front door of the White House.

It read:

DEAR DICK AND PAT,

The key is under the doormat and you can have all the food that's left in the icebox. We've tried to leave the space as spick-and-span as possible, but little Lyn was unable to find several of his toys. If you find a brown teddy bear with one eye, would you mail it to us care of the LBJ Ranch, Johnson City, Texas?

The dogs chewed up the rug on the last day, and we didn't have time to repair it, so if you folks want to have it fixed, you can send the bill to us.

The fuse box is in the cellar behind the furnace. The electric bills are outrageous, so watch the help and see that they turn out all the lights.

Garbage goes out Friday, trash on Monday; but don't mix the two, or there is a $25 fine. For example, don't throw out your budget messages with your press secretary's briefing transcripts.

The appliances are all in pretty good shape, though it gets hot in the kitchen every once in a while. You can blame Harry Truman for that. He knew about the problem, but every time someone wanted to do something about it, he said, "If you can't stand the heat, get out of the kitchen."

Lady Bird's left a list of handymen to call if you need anything repaired. If you call the plumber and tell him you're the President of the United States, he'll be over within forty-eight hours. The electrician might take a little longer, but he lives in Bethesda, Maryland, and usually doesn't make house calls.

Structurally, I think you'll find the building itself in fairly good condition, with one exception. When we first moved in, we found hordes of newspapermen coming out of the walls of the West Wing of the White House. We called the exterminators, and they did everything—they sprayed them, laid out poison bait for them, set mouse traps, and even plugged up all the leaks and holes. But the newspapermen just kept multiplying.

In the last year Lady Bird and I decided to ignore them, and I'd advise you to do the same. Trying to get rid of them seems to do more damage to the house than letting them gnaw on the foundations of your administration.

The pool should be backwashed twice a week. Marvin Watson used to do it for me before I made him Postmaster General. If you don't want to do it yourself, you can probably get Wally Hickel to do it for you. After all, he owes you a favor.

You don't have too many neighbors around you, but we solved the problem by inviting people over for lunch and dinner. The only time we ran into trouble is when we invited a bunch of artists and writers over to the house and they started passing around a petition saying they only came to eat with us to show their contempt for what we were doing in Vietnam. It kind of hurt to see them eat my groceries.

There are a bunch of trees and bushes in the garage that Lady Bird never did get a chance to plant, and she said Pat could have them. She also left the silver shovel for Pat.

I guess that's pretty much it. I think you'll like the house. It has a *je ne sais quoi* quality to it that's hard to explain.

The only advice I have is don't get too attached to the place. The landlords are pretty fickle people, and no matter what you do for them, if they take a dislike to you, they'll kick you out when your four-year lease is up.

Sincerely,
LYNDON

NIXON'S FIRST PRESS CONFERENCE

I was present at President Nixon's first press conference. A President's first press conference is as important to the press as it is to the President. The entire country is watching to see if the White House correspondents are up to questioning their leader.

About 500 of us were crouched at the West Wing starting line thirty minutes before the conference began. At the signal from the Secret Service, we made the outdoor dash for the White House portico. Running and jogging are not permitted, but the pace is fast. The reason for speed is that there are only 300 seats in the East Room, and if you're not quick enough, a woman reporter will beat you to a seat.

The idea of covering a televised Presidential press conference is to get on TV, so your family, as well as your bosses, back home will see you. The best way to do this is to ask a question, preferably a long one, so the camera will stay on you, instead of the President.

The next best thing to asking a question is to sit behind someone who you are sure will ask one.

During President Kennedy's administration I always tried to get a seat behind May Craig. It was a sure way of getting on TV. Unfortunately other reporters knew this, too, and there was always a fight for seats behind where May Craig placed herself.

In the Johnson administration we all used to gravitate behind Sarah McClendon, who writes for a string of Texas newspapers. Unfortunately, it was too early in the Nixon administration to know whom to sit behind; though after this first press conference the smart money is now on Clark Mollenhoff of the Cowles newspapers.

The ground rule for asking questions at a White House press conference is to jump up from your chair and hope the President will recognize you. That is why it's so important to have a seat. If you're already standing, the President doesn't know whether you want to ask a question or whether you were just unlucky not to get a chair.

The only thing standees can do is crouch while the President is speaking and then straighten up when he's ready to take a question and shout, "Mr. President." But it rarely works in the East Room.

Since the President of the United States cannot bestow knighthood on reporters, the next best thing is for him to recognize a newspaper reporter by name. This is comparable to Queen Elizabeth's giving someone the Order of the Garter. If the President not only recognizes someone by name, but refers to something he has written, as he did in the case of Mr. Mollenhoff, the reporter has nothing to look forward to except to be asked to leave his footprints in cement in Lyn Nugent's Children's Garden.

This was President Nixon's first press conference, and I didn't know what to do. I was tempted to sit behind Sarah McClendon on the off-chance that the change in administrations would have no effect on her being recognized. But at the last minute I decided to take a calculated risk and sit behind Edward P. Morgan, the TV and radio commentator. As luck would have it, I made the right decision, because Miss McClendon was never recognized and Mr. Morgan not only got the nod from President Nixon, but asked the longest question of the press conference. By sticking my head around Mr. Morgan's elbow, I must have been on TV for at least a minute.

I thought my father would be very happy with the exposure, but when I called him that night, his only comment was, "I liked you better when you sat behind Sarah McClendon."

Everyone who watches TV is a critic.

HOW THE "OLD" NIXON LOST OUT

As everyone knows, there are two Richard Nixons, the "old" Nixon and the "new" Nixon. It is not generally known that just before the Presidential campaign got under way, the two Nixons had a bitter fight at a strategy meeting in Miami Beach. The "old" Nixon was told he was no longer needed, that the Republicans had decided if they were going to win in 1968, they were going to have to go with the "new" Nixon.

"You can't do this to me," the "old" Nixon cried. "I've given the best years of my life to the party and you can't throw me out now."

A Republican strategist said gently, "We're not throwing you out, Dick, but you had your chance before and you blew it. If you blow it again, it could mean the end of the Republican Party. We can't take that chance."

"What does the 'new' Nixon know about politics?" shouted the "old" Nixon. "Does he know how to get in there and fight? Does he know how to hit them in the groin and knock them over the head? Does he know how to accuse them of being soft on Communism and squishy on Vietnam and disrespected all over the world? Can he slug it out toe to toe?"

"No, Dick, that's exactly what the Democrats expect us to do. But we're not going to play their game. We're going to talk about the forgotten man who works and pays his taxes, and we're going to talk about how wonderful it is to live in the suburbs and how nice it is to go to the seashore in the summertime."

The "old" Nixon jumped to his feet and yelled, "What kind of campaign is that? You have to go for the jugular. Nice guys finish last."

The "new" Nixon said, "Sit down, Dick, and listen carefully. This is a unique election situation. We don't have to attack the Democrats because they're going to make mincemeat out of one another. In order for Humphrey to get anywhere in the election, he's going to have to attack Lyndon Johnson's policies in Vietnam. Then to defend himself, Lyndon Johnson is going to have to attack Hubert Humphrey. Gene McCarthy will attack both of them, and all we have to do is sit back and talk about crabgrass in the United States."

"It's too risky," the "old" Nixon said. "You'll bore the heck out of the people. The public doesn't want a 'new' Nixon. They want the 'old' Nixon they used to kick around all the time. They're used to me, and they know what to expect. You throw another Nixon at them now and they'll all go out and vote for George Wallace."

One of the Republican strategists said, "Dick, you know that I have more respect for the 'old' Nixon than anybody in this room. But times have changed and we need a fresh image, someone—and I have to be frank now—who can make the voter forget the 'old' Nixon."

The "old" Nixon pointed his finger at the "new" Nixon and screamed, "He's out to get my job. Do you think he could ever get the goods on Alger Hiss or debate the cold war with Khrushchev in a kitchen or get pelted with rotten vegetables in South America? You bet your sweet life he couldn't. Now, after all I've done, old Tricky Dick is getting the heave-to from the party."

The "new" Nixon said sadly, "I'm sorry you had to bring it down to personalities, Dick. I was hoping that because of what the party means to you, you would support me and get behind me, if not for my sake, then for Ike's."

The "old" Nixon stared at the floor and one of the men said, "We still need you, Dick. You could play a big part in this election. We can use your tactics and your experience in gut fighting."

The "old" Nixon said finally, "What do you want me to do?"

"Will you become Spiro Agnew's campaign manager?"

FOR A HEALTHIER ECONOMY

One of the lines that got Richard Nixon a big hand during his 1968 campaign for the Presidency was "Rather than more people on welfare rolls, we want more people on payrolls."

No one argued with this statement—except possibly Nixon's economic advisers. While the Republican candidate was promising more jobs for the people, his economic advisers kept insisting we were going to have to have a lot

more unemployment if we were going to prevent inflation
and a recession.

I talked to an independent economist the other day,
Professor Ulrich Upgraph, who runs the nonprofit
Economic Health Institute:

"Professor, Richard Nixon says that we have to get
people off the welfare rolls and onto the payrolls if we
want a healthy economy. How do you feel about this?"

"Terrible," Professor Upgraph said. "Everyone knows
that when you have full employment, you have inflation,
which causes a recession, which causes more unemployment in the end."

"Then what you're saying is you need a healthy unemployment rate to have a healthy economy."

"Of course. Any fool knows that. When the unemployment rate goes below four percent, then the inflation rate
goes up five percent. The only way to stop the economy
from overheating is to slow it down, and the best way to
slow an economy down is to have four or five million
people out of work."

"That seems hard to believe."

"Look, stupid, if you have full employment, then you
have a shortage of labor, and that means labor demands
pay raises. This causes prices to go up and naturally
causes inflation."

"I know I'm dense about economic affairs, Professor,
but what I don't understand is how you can get people off
the welfare rolls onto the payrolls if you have to increase
the rate of unemployment."

"You raise a very interesting question," Upgraph said,
"particularly when everyone is so mad at so many people
being on welfare. The answer is that you have to find jobs
for people and *then* lay them off so that you don't have a
booming economy running away from itself. My solution
is to change the name 'welfare' to something else, like
'economic health insurance.' Nobody will get angry if
someone else is collecting economic health insurance. It's
the word 'welfare' that is causing all the trouble."

"But it's still the same thing, Professor," I said. "You
have the government paying people for not working,
which gets the people who are working and paying taxes
very upset."

"Ah, yes, but you must think of this in agricultural

terms. We pay farmers *not* to grow crops to keep down the surplus, and no one is too upset by that. If we pay people *not* to work to keep down inflation, it will be the same thing."

"That's true," I said. "But what are the people who aren't working going to do during the day with their time?"

"That's not an economist's problem. The sociologists have to wrestle with that one. We deal only in statistics."

"You make a strong case for unemployment, Professor, and heaven knows we need some, if we don't want more unemployment later on. But it seems to me that the more unemployment you have, the more money the government will have to spend to take care of the people. And the more debt we get into, the more unhealthy the economy will be."

Professor Upgraph said angrily, "Nobody's perfect."

SORE LOSER

In almost every election in the United States (except where someone ran unopposed) there is a winner and a loser, and American tradition demands that the loser show good grace and make a concession speech. But what he says and what he is thinking at the moment is not necessarily the same thing.

Thanks to the exact science of extrasensory perception, I am able to reveal what a candidate was thinking while he was making his concession speech on the networks early Wednesday morning after election day. He began:

"First, I want to thank all the people who worked so hard and so long in my campaign for nothing and who believed in me, and what I stood for."

But he was thinking: *If I had to do it all over again, I would have hired a professional outfit that would have at least known what the hell we were doing.*

"I can't praise too highly my campaign manager, Hiram Hathaway, who worked tirelessly on my behalf at great sacrifice to himself and his family."

All he made me promise him was a federal judgeship if I won.

"I would also like to say that I know that although my wife, Betty, is disappointed, I doubt if I could have got through the past year without her loyalty and love and understanding."

She told me from the start I didn't have a chance, and as far as she was concerned, I was nuts even to get into the race.

"As far as my opponent is concerned, I wish to congratulate him on the victory which he won fairly and squarely."

In one of the dirtiest campaigns in political history.

"I know that he will serve his state and country to the best of his ability, and I shall do everything in my power to support him in the great problems he will have to deal with in the perilous times ahead."

That is, if he isn't indicted in the next year for vote fraud.

"I would be less than candid if I didn't admit that I was disappointed in the results. But in this great country we can't all be winners, and I shall continue to serve the public in any capacity that is demanded of me."

It's going to be interesting to see who makes up my one-million-dollar campaign deficit.

"I might mention at this time how grateful I am to the press, who treated me fairly and called the shots as they saw them."

I never saw such a bunch of prejudiced, lying bunch of hacks in my life. They couldn't write the truth if it was shoved down their throats.

"As for television, I'd like to say how grateful I am to the TV stations who provided me with free time to tell my side of the story."

At six thirty in the morning.

"It's true I didn't have as much money as my opponent to buy TV time."

It pays to have a rich wife at election time, even though she's ugly as sin.

"But I don't blame the lack of money for my defeat."

Not much.

"If there were any mistakes made in this campaign, they were mine, and I must take responsibility for them."

If you believe that one, you're stupider that I thought you were.

"The important thing now is to heal the wounds and go

forward together as one people, one nation under God with liberty and justice for all."

That's not a bad phrase. I think I'll use it in the next campaign.

THE CABINET WIVES

The idea of having Cabinet wives attend President Nixon's Cabinet meetings may have several virtues, but it also has its drawbacks. Even if nothing happened at the meetings, I would still hate to be a Cabinet officer when I got home that night.

"Well," the Cabinet officer's wife says, "you hardly opened your trap during the entire meeting."

"But, dear, the President didn't call on me."

"And why, may I ask, didn't the President call on you? Your department is as important as anybody else's. I was so embarrassed with you just sitting there having nothing to say."

"It so happens that some days I do all the talking. Unfortunately, you were there on the wrong day."

"A likely story. I'm not sure the President even knows what you do. The least he could have done is let you read a report or something. If you don't have any pride, I do."

"You're overreacting. Several of the Cabinet officers didn't have anything to say either. There's only so much time in a Cabinet meeting, and we have to discuss what the President is interested in."

"Did you see the smug look on Mrs. Laird's face when her husband was explaining the Soviets' first-strike potential? And did you see Mrs. Rogers react when her husband said he didn't believe the Soviets would use it? I just had to sit there like a dummy."

"I think you've got the idea of these Cabinet meetings all wrong. The President invited the wives so they will get more interested in their husbands' jobs. I should have thought you would be intrigued with that."

"I would have, if I had found out what you did. As far as I could tell, the only contribution you made to the Cabinet meeting was to spill a pitcher of water when the Secretary of the Treasury gave his report."

"Dearest, it was an accident. Bob Finch spilled his water, and you didn't see Mrs. Finch get mad."

"I only got mad when I realized that no one had even noticed you did it. That's how much attention they were paying to you."

"You're oversensitive. Everyone in that room knows the job I'm doing."

"Then why was Mrs. Nixon staring at me as if she didn't know who I was?"

"She knew who you were. You were sitting next to me, weren't you?"

"But maybe she didn't know who you were."

"Good gravy. I didn't realize you took everything to heart. The whole point of the exercise wasn't to show one another how bright we were. We were conducting the nation's business."

"You could have said something about inflation."

"I could have said something about the ABM or the Middle East or the poverty program. But what good would it have done?"

"It would at least have let Mrs. Agnew know who you were."

"I frankly thought the meeting went pretty well."

"Well, you can say what you want to, but I'm not going to attend another one of those bring-your-wife-to-the-Cabinet-meeting sessions until I'm assured that you will ask for the floor."

"To do what?"

"To ask the President for a fresh pitcher of water, if nothing else."

HOW NIXON GOT ROCKY TO SAY NO

One of the tricks every President-elect must learn is how to offer a job to somebody in such a way that he will have to refuse it.

While Mr. Nixon spent many hours selecting his Cabinet, he spent many other hours talking to men he had no intention of hiring. One of them was Governor Nelson Rockefeller. How Mr. Nixon offered Governor Rockefeller a job without offering it to him is something we'll have to wait to find out when their memoirs are written. But until then, there is no harm in guessing.

"Nelson, it's good you could stop by. How's Happy?"

"She's very happy, Dick. Well, I guess you've got a tough job selecting the right Cabinet for the country."

"I do, Nelson. It isn't easy to find dedicated, selfless men who are willing to come to Washington and spend four years making the great decisions of history."

"Oh, it can't be that hard, Dick. I imagine there are many men who would love to serve in your Cabinet."

"Do you know of any, Nelson?"

"Well, I haven't been thinking about it much. Let me see. For Secretary of State, you ought to find someone with a prestigious name, identified with public service, with a clear, liberal image, who perhaps is the governor of a very large state."

"Exactly my thinking, Nelson. But I can't think of anyone with all these qualifications. Heaven knows, my people have looked. What about Secretary of Defense, Nelson? Do you have any ideas for me there?"

"Well, Dick, I think you ought to find someone with a prestigious name, identified with public service, with a clear, liberal image, who perhaps is the governor of a very large state."

"I'd rather have Volpe for Secretary of Transportation."

"I wasn't thinking of Volpe, Dick."

"Well, Reagan's out of the question. If I put Finch in the Cabinet as HEW Secretary, I can't put Reagan in, too."

"I wasn't thinking of Reagan, either."

"Then whom were you thinking of, Nelson?"

"I wasn't thinking of anybody. I was trying to answer your question."

"How's Happy, Nelson?"

"You asked me that before. She's fine. Who have you got in mind for Secretary of the Treasury?"

"I was going to ask you about that, Nelson. Whom do you think I ought to get?"

"I think you ought to find someone with a prestigious name, identified with public service, someone with a clear, liberal image, who perhaps is governor of a very large state."

"How about your brother David?"

"He's not a governor."

"Incidentally, Nelson, how's Happy?"

"Look, Dick, I have to get back to Albany. Is there anything else you want to ask me about?"

"Well, frankly, Nelson, I'd like you to be on my team, and there is one key job that everyone is going to be watching so far as my appointments go."

"Anything you say, Dick."

"You remember when President Johnson appointed his secretary's husband to the Subversive Activities Board and the squawk that went up?"

"I sure do."

"That job is open, Nelson, and I thought that if you would consider—"

"I'm sorry, Dick. I like my job as governor of a very large state. It's prestigious. It identifies me with public service and gives me a clear, liberal image. I wouldn't think of coming to Washington in a million years."

PROTECTING OUR MISSILES

President Nixon decided to deploy the antiballistic missile system around strategic missile sites in this country rather than around the cities. The reason he gave for his decision is that there was no possible way of protecting the cities. The next best thing was to safeguard the missile sites so that they could be used to retaliate against anyone who could be stupid enough to attack us.

The question that has probably crossed some people's minds is: What has been protecting these missile sites in the past? And the answer to the question, I can say without violating security, is police dogs. Each missile site had ten police dogs assigned to it to protect it from being attacked.

Now, admittedly, it's quite a jump from a police dog system of defense to a billion-dollar antiballistic missile defense around the sites; but this is a decision that can only be made by the President, and I'd be the last to question it.

At the same time, it's not too early to ask what effect this decision will have on the military-canine complex.

One of the most important suppliers of canines to the military said that President Nixon's decision to replace his dogs with atomic warhead missiles came as a shock.

"I think the President has overreacted. I could conceive

of his phasing out the dogs if he didn't think they were providing enough security around the sites, but having them replaced with rockets is going a bit far."

"But," I said, "the President told us one of his reasons for installing an ABM defense around missile sites was to protect them from the Red Chinese."

"Our dogs did the same thing, and much cheaper. There wasn't a Chinaman that got within five miles of an ICBM site without being sniffed out."

"Of course," I said, "the President is leaving his options open. He is also concerned about the Soviets building an ABM system. He said he probably would have been satisfied with having the sites guarded by police dogs except the Soviets had made so many gains in missiles that we couldn't stand still."

"Then why didn't he increase the number of police dogs around each Minuteman base?"

"That would have been interpreted by the Soviets as an offensive move. The President wanted to make sure the Russians understood that his building of ABM's around ICBM sites was a defensive gesture that would not be a threat to them."

"Are you trying to tell me that if the President announced he was doubling the canine protection around the Minuteman sites, the Soviets would have been tempted to escalate the arms race?"

"You seem to forget that the Russians have police dogs, too. Of course, the ideal would be to reach an agreement with the Soviets so that neither an ABM system nor a police dog guard was necessary. But that's hardly likely with the Chinese in the picture."

"Well, all I can say," said the canine supplier bitterly, "is that we know police dogs around the sites can work. But there isn't one person yet who can prove the ABM system works. I'd like to see what a computer does the next time a Chinaman tries to sneak into a Minuteman base."

SAVE THE DRAFT

I went over to my neighbor's house the other day and found his twenty-one-year-old son, Jimmy, in the garage working on picket signs which read SAVE THE DRAFT,

DOWN WITH NIXON'S PROFESSIONAL ARMY and KEEP OUR
BOYS 1-A.

You could have knocked me over with a cattle prod,
because Jimmy had been the most violent critic of the
draft in the neighborhood and had attended every Dr.
Spock rally in the country.

"What happened?" I asked him.

"I wised up," Jimmy said. "Nixon's plan to do away
with the draft and have a professional army is the biggest
fraud perpetrated on the American people. Either that or
he doesn't realize what he's doing."

"What do you mean?"

"When Nixon first said he was going to do away with
the draft, I was all for him. But then it hit me. What
would the consequences of this be? He organizes a professional army and gets excellent pay for them. The people
who are attracted to the military life join in droves and
you have the best-trained, most devoted, most dedicated
Army, Navy, and Air Force in the world."

"What's wrong with that?"

"Nothing, at the beginning. But what happens ten years
from now? The professional army is completely alienated
from the population. They sit around their barracks and
officers' clubs grousing about the civilians who don't know
a damn thing about military affairs. Finally, a bunch of
colonels get together and say, 'We don't have to take guff
from the civilians. We got the hardware. If they don't
listen to us, we'll just have to damn well make them
listen.' "

"Jimmy, you're not saying that they'd pull a military
coup d' état?"

"Why not? How many tanks does it take to surround
the White House? How many flights would you have to
make over NBC, CBS, and ABC in a fighter plane before
they'd cave in? Even the *Pueblo* could capture Washington."

"You've been reading *Seven Days in May*," I said
accusingly.

He denied it. "Do you know why this country is still a
democracy despite the fact it has the largest military
machine in the world?"

"I would hate to guess."

"Because it has thousands and thousands of draftees in

the service who *hate* it. The more people you have in the service who hate it, the less chance you will ever have of the military taking over. When you pay draftees nothing, treat them miserably, and make them sorry they ever had to put on a pair of fatigues, you've got a built-in fail-safe against anyone ever helping the professional Army officers set up a military dictatorship."

"I hate to say this, Jimmy, but you make a pretty good argument for continuing the draft."

"The worst part of it is, the military had us suckered in. When we were holding all those antidraft demonstrations, we were really helping their cause. Every time Dr. Spock made a speech, the colonels were chortling."

"So now you're going to organize prodraft demonstrations throughout the country."

"You bet your sweet General Hershey we are. The beauty of it is that they can't arrest us for demonstrating *for* the draft. Even the Daughters of the American Revolution have to be on our side."

"It's going to be a blow to J. Edgar Hoover when he hears the news," I said. "What specifically made you see the light?"

"Greece," he said as he started on a new sign—HELL YES—THE DRAFT IS BEST.

4

God Bless You,
Mrs. Robinson

CRISIS *AT* PERFECT HAPPINESS

The editors of *Perfect Happiness* were sitting around the editorial room the other day in despair.

"Our circulation figures are down; housewives are turning off on us by the thousands. What are we going to do?" one of the editors said.

"Our problem is that we're a magazine devoted to the home, and the magazines that are selling these days are those devoted to sex. Our readers would never stand for our discussing sex in a family magazine."

"Wait a minute," the art director said. "They wouldn't stand for it if we came out *for* it, but what if we had an issue devoted to coming out *against* it?"

"I don't get you."

"Suppose the theme of the issue is titled 'The Sexual Revolution Is Ruining America'?"

"What about it?"

"Don't you see—it would be an excuse to use any artwork we wanted."

"Hey," said an executive editor, "that sounds great. We could say we feel it's our duty as a leader of the mass media to show the American mother what dangers await her children in a permissive society."

"Right. We could get offensive still pictures from *I Am Curious* (*Yellow*) and *The Killing of Sister George*."

"What about a spread on the Broadway musical *Hair,* showing those horrible nude bodies on the stage?"

"Maybe we could get some photographs from *Che,* the Off-Off-Broadway show they closed up after one performance."

"We could do a montage of all the dirty movie advertisements."

Everyone was excited. "We'll get research to dig up salacious passages from *Portnoy's Complaint, Couples* and *Myra Breckenridge*."

"The food editor could do a feature on aphrodisiac foods and the dangers of them."

"Don't forget fashions," someone shouted. "We could show the topless look and the bottomless look, and how fashion designers have destroyed the clothes industry."

The editor seemed pleased. "Of course, to balance the artwork, we'd have to have some articles from respectable people who are as shocked about the sexual revolution as we are."

"What about Everett Dirksen, Dr. Norman Vincent Peale, and Al Capp?"

"That's a great idea. We ought to get a few psychiatrists and one Negro writer, too, just so people won't think that only white people are concerned about sex."

"Oh, boy," said the photo editor, clapping his hands together, "what an issue. I can't wait to get my camera."

The managing editor said, "I think if we showed a couple in the front of the book making love, it would hit our readers harder and make them aware of the frightening things that are going on in this country."

"I'm ahead of you, Peabody. I was thinking of using the couple on the cover."

"The cover," said the art director gleefully. "Oh, boy, that will really hit home."

The executive editor said, "All we're doing is showing the horrors of the sexual revolution. We don't want our readers to get any enjoyment out of this issue. Our slogan is still 'You May Not Like It, but the American Woman Has a Right to Know.' "

HOW TO BAKE A SUNDAY PAPER

Winter is the time of year when, because of inclement weather and bad pitches by groggy newsboys, your Sunday newspaper may arrive in a wet or soggy condition. Most people get angry at this state of affairs, mainly because they don't know how to dry and bake a good Sunday paper. Once you know how to do this, you may never fear getting a wet newspaper again.

My recipe for baking a newspaper was handed down in my family from one generation to the next, and even on the rainiest, snowiest, sleetiest day our family always has had the crispiest, tastiest Sunday newspaper on the block.

As a public service, it is my intention to pass on this family recipe to my loyal and devoted readers.

First, preheat oven to 300 degrees.

While you're doing that, drain off liquid from the paper and put aside.

Now get a sharp knife and start peeling off the sections of paper—the front section, then the society, sports, comics, and so forth. Wipe each section lightly with a damp cloth, and roll to even out.

By this time your oven should be hot. If it isn't, you can study the wet football scores or the classified advertisements.

Once your oven is hot enough, arrange the sections of the newspaper on the racks of the oven, but make sure they do not touch one another or get in the way of the oven door.

NOTE: It is always best to put the comics on the lowest shelf so the color does not drip down on the black-and-white pictures of Jackie Onassis.

(If your paper is very, very large, you may have to bake it in two roastings. Therefore, select the sections you want to read first, bake them, and then, while you're reading them, stick the other sections in the oven.)

I know that the big question on your mind is how long to bake or roast a Sunday newspaper. This depends strictly on the paper. Give fifteen minutes for each pound of wet newsprint. But every five minutes, turn over the sections on the rack so that they don't get too brown. Some people prefer to cook their newspaper on a rotisserie, which keeps going around in a circle, and this is probably a faster way to do it. But the danger is that if the paper touches flame, it will go up in smoke, and that won't leave you much to do on Sunday morning.

After you've allowed your newspaper first to simmer, then to stew, and finally to bake, you can test it to see if it's ready to be read. Take out the travel section or the book review, and hold it in both hands. If the paper seems firm and stays up stiff of its own accord, it's ready. On the other hand, if it sags or falls apart while you're holding it, put the rest of it back in the oven for at least another ten minutes.

Sometimes people make a mistake and overcook their

paper. You'll know your Sunday paper is too well done if it gets black around the edges and has a funny smell to it.

Your Sunday paper can be served either hot or cold to your family and can also be sliced very thin or very thick, depending on how you like it.

If you want to read it cold, transfer to a cool, dry place, and let stand fifteen minutes.

The important thing to remember is that *anyone* can bake a Sunday newspaper. All you need for the ingredients are newsprint, rain, slush or snow, a hot oven, and patience.

One more thing: There may be times when the news is so depressing that you're sorry you took the trouble to bake your paper. If this happens, just pour some cognac on it, light it, and make it into a *flambé*.

A BAD YEAR FOR MOTHERS

Nineteen sixty-nine, according to the Chinese calendar, is the "year of the rooster." In the United States it has been called the "year of the mother." It is my prediction that mothers are in for a bad time. *Portnoy's Complaint,* the Philip Roth book, does the most devastating job on a mother in modern literature, and while it's true that she's a Jewish mother, it is a known fact that most American mothers are really Jewish mothers at heart.

My Aunt Sophie in Brooklyn is very disturbed about this turn of events.

"I knew they'd get around to us sooner or later," Aunt Sophie said.

"What do you mean, Aunt Sophie?"

"First they blamed the government for all the trouble in the country; then they blamed the Vietnam War; then they blamed the schools; and finally, they've gotten down to the nitty-gritty and they're blaming us. If it wasn't for mothers, they're saying, the world would be a better place to live in."

"You shouldn't take this personally, Aunt Sophie. It's true that Philip Roth's fictional mother is very tough on her son, but that doesn't mean that every mother is like her."

"Then why is it a best seller? You think the people read the book because the hero is such a schmo? They read it because the mother is such a horrible woman and they can identify with her."

"That's just your interpretation, Aunt Sophie. Americans revere their mothers. Don't you remember we fought World War II just so we could get a hunk of Mom's apple pie?"

"Big deal. That was World War II. Now we're the guilt makers of the world. Every time you pick up the paper, you read about some horrible crime, and the psychiatrist says the one who did it had a lousy mother.

"The kids riot at the colleges, and the sociologists say they're not revolting against the school. They're really revolting against their mothers. How do you think that makes us feel?"

"Terrible, I should think," I told my Aunt Sophie. "And it is true that there is a campaign on against mothers, but I would attribute it to the confused society we're living in. People have to blame somebody for their anxieties."

"Why don't they blame John Lindsay?"

"They do, Aunt Sophie, but he gets blamed for so many things that people are getting tired of it. Do you think your son Leo blames you for all his troubles?"

"What troubles?" Aunt Sophie asked sharply.

"I didn't mean troubles. I meant the fact that Leo still isn't married."

"I've never stood in Leo's way. As a matter of fact, I'm as interested in him getting married as he is. Every night at dinner I say to him, 'When are you getting married?' Does that sound as if I'm standing in his way?"

"It certainly doesn't."

"Can I help it if he's never been able to find someone who can cook as well as I can? The girl who gets my Leo gets gold."

"What did Leo say about Philip Roth's mother?"

"I wouldn't let him read such garbage," Aunt Sophie said. "Mark my words, mothers are in for a bad period. There are going to be a lot of other books written about mothers, and none of them are going to look like Whistler's."

"You may have a point, Aunt Sophie. But I want to assure you that I will never make fun of mothers. They're the salt of the earth."

"As far as I know, you and Leo are the only ones who feel that way."

TEARS FOR WILLIE MAE

I walked into the kitchen of a friend of mine and found her crying.

"What on earth's the matter, Clara?" I asked.

"They won't let Willie Mae Rogers of *Good Housekeeping* be the President's consultant on Consumer Affairs."

"That was a disappointment to me also, Clara, but I didn't think you would take it so hard."

"But if she doesn't take the job, who will protect the consumer?"

"President Nixon will find somebody else—perhaps from *McCall's* or the *Ladies' Home Journal* or *Seventeen*."

"It isn't the same thing," Clara said, blowing her nose. "Willie Mae Rogers believed in us. I wouldn't buy anything unless it was approved by *Good Housekeeping*."

"Clara, I don't want to disillusion you, but the only products that *Good Housekeeping* approved were those that advertised in the magazine. If you didn't advertise, you didn't get the approval seal."

"It doesn't matter. *Good Housekeeping* would never accept an advertisement unless they approved of the product."

"How do you know that?"

"Because Willie Mae said so. If you can't believe in the *Good Housekeeping* Seal of Approval, what can you believe in?"

"Clara, get hold of yourself. Willie Mae would have certainly made a wonderful consultant on consumer affairs, but there was a conflict of interest."

"You see, she insisted on keeping her job at *Good Housekeeping*, and there were some Congressmen who felt if she had to divide her loyalties between the magazine and the President, the consumer might come out on the short end."

"They can say that. But there is nothing more American than being approved by *Good Housekeeping*, and Willie Mae said in her press conference that she was basically honest, so there couldn't possibly have been a conflict of interest."

"I know that and you know that, Clara, but there are always doubters and wave makers. For example, Willie Mae Rogers testified against the truth-in-packaging bill which was supposed to protect the consumer. Some of these Congressmen felt she was on the side of the advertisers."

"She couldn't be," said Clara, starting to cry again. "I saw her on television, and she didn't look as if she was on the side of the advertisers at all. Oh, what will happen to us now?"

"Clara, Clara, you have to get away from this personality cult. Our government was set up so that no one would be indispensable. There must be hundreds of Willie Mae Rogerses in this country."

"But none of them have the *Good Housekeeping* Seal of Approval."

"Look at it this way, Clara. If Willie Mae were working for the President, she wouldn't be able to devote her full time to *Good Housekeeping*, and if she weren't testing it, a product might slip through that really didn't deserve the seal. You wouldn't want that to happen, would you?"

"No," said Clara, biting on her handkerchief.

"It may be better for the country and the President if Willie Mae stays at *Good Housekeeping*, where the real consumer protection work in this country is being done."

"I hadn't thought of it that way. But maybe you're right," said Clara. "At least I can sleep better at night knowing Willie Mae is still in the *Good Housekeeping* kitchen, where she belongs."

"I think President Nixon is sleeping better, too, Clara."

HOW I GREW A MUSTACHE AND FOUND HAPPINESS

Last summer on the beautiful island of Martha's Vineyard off Cape Cod, I made one of the most important decisions of my life. I decided to grow a mustache.

I'm not quite sure why I made the decision, though I believe it had to do with the fact that I wanted to do something daring, and since I have a very jealous wife, growing a mustache is about as daring as she'll let me get. Little did she know what she was getting in for.

It wasn't the first time I had extra hair on my face. About ten years ago I had gone on safari in Africa and had grown a beard in true Hemingway tradition. Unfortunately, it started to itch after a while and I shaved it off.

I thought that since I had once grown a beard, a mustache would present fewer problems, but I was absolutely wrong. Once you decide to grow a mustache, there are many questions to be faced. The most important, of course, is what kind of mustache to grow? I knew I didn't want a thin one over the lip since that kind is usually identified with French waiters and unpleasant hotel managers. I didn't want a Sergeant Pepper mustache since I would be accused by my children of identifying with the Beatles. A handlebar mustache intrigued me, though I was afraid it would take too long to grow, and I wanted results immediately. So I finally settled for a full brush-type mustache, which I'll have to admit I modeled after Joseph Stalin, whose biography I was reading at the time. (Let J. Edgar Hoover make the most of this if he wants to.)

Once the decision had been made, I started to let the mustache grow. The most painful time for anyone growing a mustache is the first week.

It isn't quite a mustache, and it isn't quite not a mustache. During these early stages one has to put up with the worst kinds of remarks from so-called friends, such as, "You have some dirt above your lip." "You forgot to shave under your nose this morning." "What did you do, lose an election bet?" and "Heil Hitler."

Unless you're strong, you can easily be discouraged during this time. Fortunately for me, just when I became the most discouraged, I discovered that I could darken the mustache with my wife's mascara, so it looked like a much better mustache than it was.

The only one who detected this deceit was a six-year-old daughter of a friend of mine, who declared in front of a full room, "You put black crayon all over your mustache."

During the second week the mustache started to take on some body, and I didn't have to resort to as much mascara, and by the third week the mustache had thickened to the point where I didn't have to fake it at all.

Then the fun began. The mustache was the immediate topic of conversation at every party on Martha's Vineyard. While the men thought it was a good joke, I noticed that some of their wives seemed to be very intrigued with the addition to my face, and I became the center of attraction to many ladies who wouldn't give me the right time of day in the past.

"Why did you do it?" a lady would ask.

"Because it's sexy," I would reply.

There would be a laugh, but she wasn't quite sure if I was kidding or not.

So then came the challenge: "Why is it more sexy?"

"Because," I would explain patiently in tones that I imagined Errol Flynn once used, "a mustache adds something to a kiss."

Nervous laughter from the ladies.

"I'm not kidding," I would say. "The reason why women don't like mustaches is that most men when kissing them hit them head on and it's like suddenly being smacked on the lips with a brush. The secret of kissing with a mustache is to rub the mustache softly across a woman's cheek, back and forth, grazing so it just touches the skin, causing goose pimples to start from the toes and ascend upward. Would you like me to demonstrate?"

No more laughter—just nervousness. "Oh, well, go ahead if you want to."

I would then proceed to illustrate my point. Staying away from her lips, I would graze her cheek, inevitably causing chills, blushes, and occasional looks of fear and surprise. In almost every instance I won my case.

I'm not one to brag, but in three weeks I became one of the most sought-after guests on Martha's Vineyard. Women stopped me in the supermarket in hopes I would kiss them on the cheek; others would greet me on the beach with open arms; still other women sought to play tennis with me in hopes I would kiss them after the game was over. And all the time their stupid husbands were laughing at me.

All the attention and success started to go to my head, and I imagine I was getting hard to live with because my personality was starting to change. From a round little Mr. Milquetoast I had suddenly been transformed into a five-foot-eight Cesar Romero, and my wife didn't seem to be enjoying it one bit.

The first time she protested I said, "The other women are just getting a taste of the mustache while you're getting the full benefit of it."

"That may be, lover boy," she replied. "But if I have to give up this added pleasure to defend my home, I'm going to do it."

"You mean you want me to shave it off?"

"You can keep it for two more weeks since you worked so hard on letting it grow. Then it goes or I go."

It was like telling a man he had only two more weeks to live. I pleaded with her, promising her I wouldn't demonstrate it anymore. I told her I needed it for my ego and for all the wasted years of my youth.

But my pleas fell on deaf ears. "Two weeks," she said. "And make the best of it."

I should have shaved it off the next morning because when I knew it would have to go in two weeks, my heart wasn't in my work anymore. All I could think about was how many disappointed women there would be once my vacation was over.

You can guess the rest of the story. I'm back to where I was before I went to Martha's Vineyard. I sit alone at parties; women walk by me without giving me a second glance; instead of grazing, I shake hands. And every morning, as I look in the mirror and start putting shaving cream on my upper lip, I can't help thinking of what might have been. It's enough to make a forty-year-old man cry.

SEX ED—THE PROS AND CONS

There is a big flap going on in the United States right now over the question of teaching sex education in our schools. The educators are mostly for it and the ultraconservatives, including the John Birchers and the DAR, are mostly against it. I usually like to stay out of controversial matters since I hate to answer my mail, but in this case I have to come out for teaching sex education in the schools.

This is a very personal matter with me. I had no formal sex education when I was a student, and everyone knows the mess I'm in. If there had been a Head Start program in sex education when I was going to public school, I might have been a different man today.

When I was going to Public School 35 in Hollis, New York, we got all our sex education at the local candy store after three o'clock. The information was dispensed by thirteen-year-olds who seemed to know everything there was to know on the subject, and we eleven- and twelve-year-olds believed every word they told us.

Some of it, I discovered later on, did not necessarily happen to be true. For example, I was told as an absolute fact that if a girl necked with you in the rumble seat of a car, she would automatically have a baby.

This kept me out of the rumble seat of an automobile until I was twenty-three years old.

There were some other canards of the day, including one that the method of kissing a girl on the mouth decided whether she would become pregnant or not. Every time I kissed a girl after that, I sweated for the next nine months.

The sex experts at Sam's Candy Store had an answer for every problem that was raised at the soda fountain. These included warnings that if you did certain things, you would go insane. Most of us were prepared to be taken off to the booby hatch at any moment.

There was obviously no talk about birds, bees, flowers, or animals. We couldn't care less what happened when *they* were doing it. Our only concern was what happened to human beings, and from what our thirteen-year-old instructors could tell us, it was all bad.

Those of us who escaped insanity and shotgun weddings were told we would probably wind up with a horrendous disease that would be passed on to our children and their children for generations to come. There were twenty-five ways of catching this disease, including shaking hands with someone who knew someone who had it.

You can imagine the nightmares these tales produced. There seemed to be no escape. You were doomed if you did, and you were doomed if you didn't. After one of these sessions at the candy store, I seriously contemplated suicide. There didn't seem to be any other way out.

Now the worst part of my sex indoctrination was that when I turned thirteen, I became an instructor myself and passed on my knowledge to eleven- and twelve-year-olds at the same candy store. They listened in awe as I repeated word for word what I had been told by my "teachers," and I was amazed with how much authority I was able to pass on the "facts" of sex education as I knew them.

Upon becoming thirteen, they in turn taught the younger students. Heaven knows how many generations of Public School 35 alumni went on through life believing everything they had learned about sex at Sam's Candy Store.

The fact is that while the sex education at Sam's served a purpose, we were all emotional wrecks before we got to high school.

So, on the basis of my own experience, I don't think we have much choice in this country when it comes to sex education. In order to avoid the agony and pain my fellow classmates and I went through, we either have to teach sex in the schools or close down every soda fountain in the United States.

GOD BLESS YOU, MRS. ROBINSON

In the movie *The Graduate,* the hero, Dustin Hoffman, is seduced by a Mrs. Robinson. Thanks to a hit song written and sung by Simon and Garfunkel, "Mrs. Robinson" has now become part of American folklore. I hadn't realized the impact of the film or the song until I started talking with a friend who happened to have the same name.

This Mrs. Robinson, a middle-aged lady, said that because of *The Graduate,* she's had a new lease on life.

"I didn't realize what was going on at first," she said. "But then one day as I paid my bill at the grocer's with a check, the young man behind the counter winked at me and started singing, 'Jesus loves you more than you will know—wo, wo, wo.'

"A few days later, as I was getting gas for my car, I handed over my credit card, and when the young man looked at it, he whistled and said, 'Where are you going tonight, Mrs. Robinson?'

"At first I was going to complain to the manager, but then I thought to myself, *If I got two passes in one week, there must be something more to this than I'm aware of.*

"I discovered what was up when my teen-age son said, 'All the guys want to meet you, Mom.'

" 'What on earth for?'

"He just laughed and said, 'Heaven holds a place for those who pray—hey, hey, hey. Hey, hey, hey.'

"I got mad and said, 'Stop this drivel. What's going on with you kids these days?'

"He brought down the Simon and Garfunkel record and said, 'Coo coo ca-choo, Mrs. Robinson.' "

Mrs. Robinson continued:

"When I heard the record, I was flabbergasted, and when I went to see the movie *The Graduate*, I was dumbfounded. I wondered how many Mrs. Robinsons were being defamed because of one Mrs. Robinson who had gone astray."

"What could you do about it without changing your name?" I said.

"I gave it some thought, and I decided the worst thing to do was fight it. So now when the grocery boy winks at me, I wink back, and when the gas station attendant starts getting fresh, I just start singing, 'Where have you gone, Joe DiMaggio, a nation turns its lonely eyes on you, ooo, ooo, ooo.' "

"What about your son's friends?"

"They're around the house all the time. Before the film came out, they never talked to me. Now they invite me to join all their conversations, and they are interested in everything I have to say."

"What does Mr. Robinson have to say about all this?"

"That's the amazing thing. With all this hubbub going on with the kids, he's suddenly taken a new interest in me, and for the first time in ten years he's jealous. Every time someone sings, 'Put it in your pantry with your cupcakes. It's a little secret—the Robinsons' affair,' he seethes with rage. It's nice still to be wanted when your kids are in high school."

"I guess in the long run, then, this has been a good year for the Mrs. Robinsons of this world."

"Let's say it was a bonus that none of us expected. God bless you please, Simon and Garfunkel."

As I shook hands with her, an amazing thing happened. For the first time I noticed that Mrs. Robinson looked very attractive, almost, I might say, beautiful.

"Well, good-bye," she said in a lovely, lilting voice.

Somehow the magic had worked. As I walked away, I started singing, "What's that you say, Mrs. Robinson? Joltin' Joe has left and gone away. Hey, hey, hey. Hey, hey, hey."

WHEN DISSENT GOES TOO FAR

In the wild age of dissent we're living in, there should be no surprises. But I was flabbergasted to read that about 100 women had picketed the Miss America Pageant in Atlantic City against "ludicrous beauty standards that had enslaved the American women." Carrying signs deploring the "degrading, mindless boob-girlie system," the pickets also set up ashcans into which they threw girdles, lipstick, hair curlers, false eyelashes, and wigs. The final and most tragic part of the protest took place when several of the women publicly burned their brassieres.

As one who has always been on the side of protesters, I regret to say that I believe this demonstration in Atlantic City has gone too far. It is one thing to protest against a system or an institution, but it is another to take the law into your own hands and burn your bra.

By demanding that women do away with all beauty aids, including false eyelashes, wigs, hair tints, girdles, and the like, so they will be on an equal footing with men, these well-meaning but misled females were trying to destroy everything this country holds dear.

It is a known fact that the American woman, beautiful though she is, needs all the help she can get. For years now hundreds of thousands of scientists and billions of dollars in research have gone into new methods of making the American female the most attractive, the most seducible, the most irresistible woman in the world. Where nature failed, American know-how succeeded, and thanks to our scientific ingenuity, it is now impossible for anyone to know where God leaves off and Maidenform takes over.

These well-meaning pickets believe that by doing away with all the beauty "hardware" that is so necessary to the American women, they will gain freedom and sexual independence.

The opposite, of course, is true. The American male is

so intent on getting ahead in the U.S. economic society, that despite all the aids a woman now uses, he hardly pays any attention to her.

If the average American female gave up all her beauty products she would look like Tiny Tim, and there would be no reason for the American male to have anything to do with her at all.

The protesters think they're bringing about a revolution by discarding all feminine makeup, but actually they're turning back the clock to precivilization days, when men and women did look and smell alike. In those days, if we're to believe the cave-dwelling drawings, men did nothing but club women over the head. It was only after the women started rubbing rose petals on themselves and putting dust on their cheeks and red clay in their hair that the men stopped batting them around.

As we saw in Chicago, there are still many men who would like to club women over the head, if they're given the slightest excuse, and there is no better excuse for hitting a woman than the fact that she looks just like a man.

If the women in Atlantic City wanted to picket the Miss America Beauty Pageant because it is lily white, that is one thing, and if they wanted to picket because it is a bore, that is also a legitimate excuse.

But when they start asking young American women to burn their brassieres and throw away their false eyelashes, then we say dissent in this country has gone too far.

WHEN DO YOU SPANK YOUR WIFE?

I rarely take an interest in a divorce story, but I was intrigued by Actress Dyan Cannon's divorce suit against movie actor Cary Grant. In the course of the testimony, Mrs. Grant charged that her husband spanked her. But Mr. Grant's lawyer defended the actor by stating his client had only spanked his wife for "reasonable and adequate causes."

My mind boggled when I read this, and I immediately called my lawyer and asked him what was legally considered a "reasonable and adequate cause" for spanking one's wife.

My lawyer, one of the great legal minds of this country,

said, "This is the seventh call I've gotten today. I didn't realize Cary Grant had such an ardent following."

"Just answer the question," I said.

"Well, each state provides 'reasonable and adequate' causes for spanking a wife but there are also general standards which are accepted in all fifty states."

"Could you give me some examples?"

"First, you must prove provocation beyond a shadow of a doubt. For example, if your wife interrupts you while you're telling a joke in mixed company, you, of course, have a right to spank her."

"Is nagging sufficient cause?"

"Not nagging per se, but if she keeps repeating herself over and over again, you can swat her."

"What if she's constantly late?"

"That goes under the heading of chronic tardiness. Tardiness was upheld in the *Conrad v. Conrad* divorce case of 1954. If you recall, Mrs. Conrad was always late when they were going out to dinner. So one night Conrad let her have it. Mrs. Conrad sued for cruelty, but lost."

"Because the judge said it was okay for Mr. Conrad to have spanked her?" I asked.

"No, because Mrs. Conrad showed up too late for the trial."

My lawyer said there were many mitigating circumstances for paddling your wife. One of the most serious was if she showed willful disregard for times when you were trying to sleep and she wanted to talk.

He added: "When you discuss spanking your wife, you must always keep in mind three guidelines: One is motive, two is intent, and three is desire. What was her motive in bugging you? How long did she intend to pursue it? And when did you desire to strike back?

"Another thing to keep in mind is how you commit the assault. In the case of Cary Grant, the testimony related he grinned when he spanked his wife. Now this was a wise thing. If you always grin when you strike your wife, you can never be accused of malice."

"Are there any other legal reasons for spanking your wife?"

"Failure to report telephone messages could be one. If she relates a confidence to a friend, you have just cause.

The most serious, though—one no judge in the land would rule against—is if she forgets to put gas in the car."

"If you're in doubt," I asked, "is it better to strike her or to check first to see if you have legitimate grounds?"

"This question comes up all the time. We usually go by the *Linseed v. Linseed* ruling of 1949, in which the judge ruled that the reason for spanking your wife is not as important as when you do it."

"I don't understand."

"The judge, in his historic *Linseed* decision, said that a wife must only be spanked reasonably close to the act of disobedience. Otherwise, she will not relate the spanking to the disobedient act. Also, the spanking must be swift, but not harsh, and you may never leave any marks. Above all else, you must smile while you're doing it."

THE CHRISTMAS PLAY

Whoever thinks the theater is dying in America probably doesn't have any children of school age. The truth is that the class Christmas play is still the hottest entertainment around. It is playing to capacity, captive holiday audiences everywhere.

I was on my way to work with my friend Renfrew one morning, and he asked me if I would mind stopping by his daughter's school. He had promised to see her in "Hark! Is That a Snowflake Falling?"—a play that the eighth grade had been working on since September 17.

Since Renfrew drives me to work on cold, wet mornings, I didn't have much choice but to say I would.

"It won't take but a few minutes," he assured me.

We went into the school auditorium, which was rapidly filling up with proud parents, though I noticed most of the fathers were anxiously looking at their watches. A teacher handed us a mimeographed program that I scanned for a few seconds, and then I said, horrified, "Renfrew, each class has its own play, starting with the kindergarten. 'Hark! Is That a Snowflake Falling?' is listed as the ninth item."

"It will go fast," he assured me. "They're very short plays."

We waited for the 9 A.M. curtain to go up, but because of some hitch, it didn't go up until 9:35.

The kindergarten did "Up the Chimney," which went for ten minutes. The first grade did a musical titled "What Angels Do We See Tonight?" with a reprise at the end. The second grade was well into "Grump, Grump, a Christmas Slump" when I turned to Renfrew and said, "It's ten thirty. I have to get to my office."

"Ursula has seen me," Renfrew whispered. "I can't go now."

"Which one is Ursula?"

"She's one of the snowflakes," Renfrew said.

"There are fifteen snowflakes."

"She's the one who's waving to me." He waved back. "It won't take long."

As each child finished the lines in his play, I noticed an anxious father jump up from his seat and dash for the door. After the third, fourth, and fifth grades had finished their presentations, the auditorium was half-empty. I like Renfrew, but I couldn't help wishing he had a child in one of the earlier grades.

The sixth grade did a mystery play, and the seventh performed "How They Got the Christmas Tree from Maine to Arizona," which required a sequence about each state en route.

It was 11:50. Only the parents of the eighth grade were still there, and one stranger who, if he had to do it all over again, would have gone to work by taxi.

Finally, "Hark! Is That a Snowflake Falling?" was ready to be performed. A hush went over the audience.

"No matter how many times I see her on the stage, I still tense up," Renfrew said.

A fairy princess came down the line of snowflakes and held her wand over Ursula's head. "And what do you want to be?"

Ursula stood up straight and blurted out, "I want to be the first snowflake on Christmas morning that any child will see."

The princess moved on.

"Okay," Renfrew said, "we can leave now."

"You got to be kidding," I said. "We sat here four hours for one line?"

"You're lucky," Renfrew said, "last year she was a church bell, and all she had to say was 'Bong.'"

As we we were driving downtown Renfrew said, "Well, tell me. What did you honestly think?"

"Renfrew," I said, patting him on the shoulder, "it was a memorable morning in the theater."

THE MAN WHO HATED BENEFITS

I am, as most people in Washington know, a very patient man. But there are times when even I lose my cool, and it usually happens in the winter when everyone is giving galas and benefits for some worthy cause.

Several months ago I came home from the office, and before I could take off my tie and splash some water on my face, my wife said, "We've been asked to go on the committee for a white tie benefit they're giving for the Indigent Football Coaches Home in Rock Creek Park. Now before you explode, Eliza Stickler, the chairwoman, said we didn't have to do any work. They just want to use our names on the invitations."

I exploded. "You know that's just a way they're going to sucker us in."

"I knew that's what you'd say, but it's a worthy cause, and it's under the patronage of Mrs. Richard Nixon, the Postmaster General, and all of Justice William Douglas' ex-wives. We really couldn't say no."

"Of course not," I shouted. "If we said no, we'd be taken out of the *Green Book,* and they'd cancel our credit at Avigone Frères."

"You're behaving ridiculously. There is nothing wrong with their using our name if it will help the home for Indigent Football Coaches."

I forgot about the whole thing until three weeks later, when my wife said to me at supper, "Who do you want to invite to the gala?"

"What do you mean, who do I want to invite to the gala?"

"Well, since we're sponsors, we have to take a table for ten so we can invite four other couples."

"How much is this little table going to cost?"

"It's two hundred dollars a couple, but before you get excited, it's deductible."

"Deductible from what?" I asked.

"I don't know," she said. "They said it was deductible, so we didn't have to worry about it."

"You know what it's deductible from?" I said. "It's deductible from the children's tuition, that's what."

"Oh, what's the difference? It's going to be a wonderful night. Eliza said they're going to have Danny Kaye, Sammy Davis, Jr., Frank Sinatra, and the Tijuana Brass for entertainment."

I ate my chipped beef and grits in silence. Two days later, right in the middle of the Washington Redskin-Baltimore game, my wife said, "Charlotte Possum just called, and she's on the raffle committee, and she said she was wondering if you'd ask Garfinckel's to donate a mink coat for the drawing."

"How can I ask Garfinckel's to donate a mink coat when we haven't even paid our bill there for two months?"

"Well, Charlotte said they'd say no to her, but if you asked and they refused, you could write a nasty article about them."

"I thought we didn't have to do anything but lend our names to the committee."

"What's wrong with asking Garfinckel's for a mink coat? Oh, by the way, I need a check for a hundred and fifty dollars."

"What for?"

"For the advertisement in the program."

"What have we got to advertise?"

"Nothing, silly. But I promised Eleanor Poolsinger—she's in charge of the program—we'd take an ad which would say 'Compliments of a Friend.' "

"You mean we can't even put our own name in the ad?"

"Now you know that would be very gauche."

Baltimore scored again, so I really can't say what depressed me the most.

The next night I came home and my wife wasn't there. We waited until eight o'clock for dinner and then opened a can of chow mein. She arrived at eight thirty. "We had a meeting of the decorations committee," she said breathlessly. "And we're going to turn the Sheraton Park Ballroom into a football stadium with gold goalposts and blue velvet-covered stands. Lillian Sollaway knows this wonderful French decorator in New York who is going to come down and do it for us."

"It sounds wonderful. You got a call from the caterer. What's that all about?"

"Oh, I forgot to tell you. The committee asked me to give a dinner party before the ball for all the African and Southeast Asia ambassadors and their wives. I think I ought to order some new drapes for the dining room."

I lost all interest in my chow mein. "This thing is kind of running into money," I said.

"A little, but it'll be fun, and you'll love the new dress I bought for the ball."

The day finally arrived, though it was hard to believe. Our dinner party of fifty was a huge success, and afterward we all went to the ball. Unfortunately Danny Kaye, Sammy Davis, Jr., Frank Sinatra, and the Tijuana Brass had previous commitments, and the entertainment was provided by a tap dancer from Hackensack, New Jersey; a singer, who was the sister of the chairwoman of the entertainment committee; and a Congressman from Texas who did card tricks.

Two weeks later, thanks to Riggs Bank, I paid off all our personal debts.

I forgot all about the gala until one night I said to my wife, "Oh, by the way, how much money did you people make for the Indigent Football Coaches Home in Rock Creek Park?"

"I think it was thirty-nine dollars and fifty cents," my wife said hesitatingly. "It seems the decorations cost us much more than anyone thought they would."

5

Who's On First?

EUROPE ACCORDING TO PEANUTS

Since everyone is so confused about what is going on in Western Europe, I think the only way to explain it is in terms of the comic strip "Peanuts."

Try to imagine that Lucy is France. She wants to be the leader of the gang, and her greatest pleasure is getting into everyone's hair.

Linus represents Great Britain, and he keeps sucking his thumb and holding a blanket which says "Made in the U.S.A."

Charlie Brown, for obvious reasons, is the United States, and every time Lucy does something to him, all he can say is "Good Grief."

Schroeder, of course, is West Germany, and Snoopy is Italy.

Long ago, Charlie Brown formed a baseball team called the NATO Defenders, and Lucy played first base. But a few years ago she got mad at Charlie Brown, quit the team, and made everyone get out of her yard. She also urged everyone else to quit, too. But the other members of the team refused, because Charlie Brown had the only bat and ball that meant anything.

Lucy, Schroeder, Snoopy, and the other kids have a club which they formed to sell lemonade to one another. Linus has been trying to join this club since it started, but Lucy said she won't let him in until he gets rid of his "Made in the U.S.A." blanket.

Linus is deathly afraid to give up his blanket because if he did, he might also have to give up his thumb sucking. Besides, Charlie Brown gave it to him for Christmas, and he doesn't want to hurt Charlie's feelings.

Last week Lucy told Linus secretly that he could come into the lemonade club if he quit Charlie Brown's team. She proposed that Linus, Schroeder, and Snoopy could be the leaders of the new club, and the rest of the gang, instead of being equal partners, could become associate club members.

Linus was horrified at Lucy's suggestion, so he told Schroeder, Snoopy, Charlie Brown, and the rest of the gang about Lucy's proposal.

Everyone was furious at Lucy for what they considered a double cross. When Charlie Brown heard the proposal he said, "Good Grief."

Schroeder said he could never leave Charlie Brown's team because there would be no one to protect him if the gang down the next street tried to steal second base.

Snoopy, who usually is very quiet, also thought Lucy's idea was a lousy one, and he had no intention of getting in the doghouse with Charlie Brown.

Lucy was furious with Linus for ratting on her, and she denied she had ever made the proposal. She also indicated that Linus would never get into the lemonade club even if he did give up his blanket, which Linus had no intention of doing.

Despite Lucy's French temper and desire to wreck Charlie Brown's team, Charlie still insists he wants to be friends with her, and he keeps asking her to come back and play ball.

But Lucy will have none of it. She says she'll play only if she's the captain and Charlie Brown sits on the bench. "I don't care if it is your ball and bat," Lucy said. "It happens to be my playing field."

Not long ago, Lucy got into trouble with her lemonade stand and made much more lemonade than she could sell. Also, her prices were so high that no one would buy it. So she immediately went to Charlie Brown and said, "You have to bail me out."

I know you're not going to believe this, but good old Charlie Brown dug into his pocket, handed Lucy the money, and all he could think of to say was "Good Grief."

PIERRE WRITES TO FRANÇOIS

PARIS—

DEAR FRANÇOIS:

I wish I could tell you things are going well here in Paris, François, but I would not be telling the truth. As you know, everyone in France keeps his gold in his mattress, and because of the recent surge in gold buying, the mattresses are so lumpy that no one has been able to get any sleep. People walk around with cricks in their backs and bruises on their arms and legs from turning over in bed. Tempers are short, and a certain *joie de vivre* has gone out of the French people.

Even my mistress, Yvonne, has been complaining. I bought so much gold last week I couldn't get it all in my mattress at home, so I asked Yvonne if she would mind if I stored some gold in *her* mattress. At first she said she wouldn't, but after a couple of nights she said either the gold had to go or she would. I hate to take Yvonne off the gold standard.

It's true, François, that all we talk about in France these days is gold. I went to the dentist the other day to have my teeth cleaned, and before I knew it, the dentist had filled every tooth in my mouth with gold. I complained, because he had told me on the previous visit that I had no cavities. But he just shrugged his shoulders and said, "I don't know what to do with the gold I've got, so I might as well fill teeth with it."

Everywhere you go it's the same story. Even in the restaurants they now sprinkle gold powder on your salad whether you ask for it or not. Several restaurants are now featuring cream of bullion soup, and instead of bacon, liver is now served with strips of gold on it.

In the grocery stores, for every bar of soap you buy, you get a free bar of gold. And if you drive into a gasoline station and you can name the President of France, they give you a free gold bumper for your car.

People are getting so fed up with having gold forced on them that they've been dumping it in junk piles at night in empty lots all over the city, which, as you can imagine, has played havoc with Madame de Gaulle's beautification program.

Employes must now accept their wages in gold, instead of checks, and many unions have protested that their members have wound up with hernias before they got home.

You remember, dear François, the barricades the students used to build at the Boulevard St.-Michel with paving stones? Well, now they are using gold bricks instead, which are infinitely cheaper.

There is even talk of tearing down the Eiffel Tower and rebuilding it in gold. Of course, President de Gaulle is aware of what the gold surplus is doing to his country, and he has ordered a crash program with French scientists to see if they can find a way to turn gold into some useful metal such as aluminum or copper. The first person to come up with such a formula will make a fortune.

In spite of all the surplus, the French speculators and government are still buying gold, and not only has this caused great hardship to us economically, but it is also changing the moral values of the French people.

Just yesterday, I bought Yvonne a solid 18-carat gold necklace with earrings and a bracelet to match, and she threw them out the window and screamed at me, "Gold, gold, gold. That's all you ever give me. Did it ever occur to you I might want rhinestones instead?"

I envy you, François. You don't have such problems in the United States right now.

Your cher ami,
PIERRE

THE AMERICAN REVOLUTION

PARIS—Ambassador and Mrs. Sargent Shriver held a July Fourth party for 1,000 French students between the ages of eight and seventeen. They asked me, as a personal favor, if I would explain the American Fourth of July in terms the French students would understand. So I'm going to try.

On July 4, 1776, a group of American students decided to overthrow the decadent colonial system of the bourgeois British. Called the Enragés of '76, the students had been furious for some time at the British educational system, the rules concerning dormitory hours for co-eds, and the insistence of the Establishment that only British tea be served in student cafeterias.

The year before, a bunch of Enragés had taken the law into their own hand, and dressed as Indians, they had boarded a ship to Boston and dumped all the tea into the harbor. This infuriated the tea merchants, who accused the Boston colonial police of being too permissive for not immediately shooting the looters and restoring law and order at the harbor.

The British, reacting strongly to criticism, decided to put the students in their place at Lexington and Concord. But the students were tipped off by a student anarchist named Paul Revere, who rode through the New England towns on a horse warning the people that the *flics* were coming.

When the British gendarmes heard about it, they trumped up charges against Revere for stealing a horse, but he escaped and became a hero of the Revolution.

In the meantime, the students had set up barricades at Bunker Hill and occupied the administration building and the library. The British *flics,* dubbed Redcoats, attacked Bunker Hill and, after much brutality, drove the Enragés out.

This act of stupidity on the part of the police turned the working class of the colonies against the Establishment, and they sent a petition to King George III demanding that he resign.

George III refused, saying if he went, there would be no one to take his place and there would be chaos and disorder in the land. He also hinted the French were behind the whole thing in an effort to embarrass him (at that time the British were attacking the French franc and buying up all the French gold).

When word was received that George III wouldn't give in on any of the Enragés' demands, though he did promise to appoint a commission to study the violence at Bunker Hill, the Committee of Revolutionists was formed with the express purpose of breaking off from the Empire.

They met in the student union at Philadelphia. One of the leaders there, Thomas Jefferson, known as White Tom because the hair in his wig was all white, drafted a Declaration of Independence, which was printed in the underground press of the time.

This made the British government officials so mad they called up the National Guard and vowed to wipe out the treasonous elements in the colonies.

But by this time the Revolution had spread to all parts of the country, and under the leadership of a wide-eyed revolutionary named George Washington, the Americans defeated the British and threw them out of the country.

And so every July Fourth the Americans celebrate the anniversary of the student revolution which changed the history of the world. The British don't talk about it, although General Cornwallis, who commanded the Redcoats, did say, when he got back to England after the war, "It would have never happened if they had invented tear gas in time."

WHO'S ON FIRST?

PARIS—The students in France may be revolting against their parents and the system, but in one respect they're really chips off the old blocks. When it comes to politics, the sons are as fragmented as their French fathers ever were.

This is how it was explained to me by a French student who was selling one of the dozens of underground newspapers that have sprung up since the events of last spring.

"The Movement of the Twenty-second of March started the ball rolling in Nanterre under the leadership of Daniel Cohn-Bendit. It was a true democratic movement in that it was in opposition to every structure, including itself. Because of this, it was able to unite various Trotskyite groups, the anarchists, the Che Guevarists and the pro-Mao revolutionaries into taking action. The action consisted of getting the masses to take to the streets. Once the masses were in the streets, the government would be forced to take counter action, which would give the students a chance to take further action, which would make the government counteract again. You're following me?"

"I think so."

"But once the action had been taken, the students started to disagree on the goals of the revolution. For example, the Federation of Student Revolutionaries, which had broken off from the Union of Communist Students because it considered the Communist Party a traitor to the cause of Communism, came out for a 'permanent revolution.' They were not concerned with student reforms, but wanted to unite with the workers in a class struggle. They thought the barricades were an exercise in futility.

"This infuriated the Young Communist Revolutionaries, who also are opposed to the French Communist Party, but helped at the barricades in spite of the fact they didn't think France was in a prerevolutionary situation, which would give them a chance to bring down the government. Their hero is Che Guevara because he started a revolutionary struggle even though the time was unfavorable. Are you still following me?"

"I'm at the barricades."

"Please do not be confused between the Young Communist Revolutionaries and the Union of Young Communists, Marxist and Leninist, who are pro-Maoist and still defend Stalin. The Union of Young Communists did not man the barricades, but instead contacted the workers in the hope of overthrowing the pro-Soviet French Communist Party. They were in fact more interested in destroying the present French Communist Party than in destroying the French government. The Union of Young Communists overplayed their hand at the Renault factory when they told the workers 'to take the flame of revolution from the students' fragile hands and carry it in their strong work-hardened fists.' This was no way to talk to workers, and they were thrown out of the factory."

"I think I'm losing you," I said.

"Then there was the Union of National Students, which was composed of students from different political complexions who united under its red banner. The Union of National Students took over the leadership of the anarchists and left-wing movements and provided the manpower for the revolution, while the Trotskyites, Stalinists, and Maoists fought amongst themselves."

"Things were simpler at Columbia University," I had to admit.

"I haven't told you about the right-wing student group called the Occident. They're the Fascists who attacked the Union of National Students which caused the fight which gave the police an excuse to occupy the Sorbonne."

"Things were even simpler at Berkeley. By the way, what ever happened to Daniel Cohn-Bendit, the fellow who started it all?"

"I don't know. Someone said he's in Switzerland going to summer school."

ONE-UPMANSHIP IN REVOLUTIONS

PARIS—All the French seem to want to talk about these days is *their* revolution. They don't have any interest at all in what has been happening in the United States, and they've been so boorish about it I've found myself bragging about our riots back home.

This is how the conversation has been going:

"You should have been here during the uprising," Anatole said. "It was fantastic."

"Maybe so," I said, "but you don't know what a riot is until you live through one in Washington, D.C."

"Ours wasn't a riot," Anatole said. "It was an all-out revolution."

"Ours could have been, except for the curfew. You didn't have a curfew in Paris, did you?"

"No, but we had a general strike," he said angrily. "You couldn't even get gasoline for your automobile."

"We had looting and burning. Whole blocks were incinerated."

"The students burned every car on the Left Bank," Anatole replied. "They also broke windows. Did you have any barricades?"

He had me there. "No, we didn't have any barricades, but we had marines and paratroopers patrolling the streets," I said. "We could have been at war."

"Our students took over all the buildings at the university," Anatole said.

"So did ours at Columbia. They gave no quarter."

Anatole toyed with his *apéritif*. Then he said, "Our police were more brutal to the students than your police."

"How can you say that?" I cried. "Our police used billy clubs and tear gas and hoses."

"Aha," said Anatole, "our police also used clubs. But they were six feet long, and the police threw the tear gas right into the students' faces. They also beat them up on the way to the station."

"Our students were also beat up. Many of them are still in jail. It sounds as if you people had a tea party."

"A tea party?" Anatole said, slamming down his drink. "We had a million people march from the Place de la République to the Sorbonne."

"We had shootings in Detroit," I said.

"But we have censorship here on the television. You at least know what's going on."

"We're afraid to walk the streets at night," I said, hoping that would put Anatole in his place.

"All the banks were on strike," Anatole said, pretending he didn't hear me. "We didn't even have any money."

"Everyone in America owns a gun," I said.

"We almost overthrew President de Gaulle," Anatole declared.

"We overthrew President Johnson."

"Ah, yes, but you did it peacefully."

"Nevertheless, we got rid of our President, and you didn't."

I could see Anatole was losing his cool, so I tried to placate him. "For a small country, you had a pretty good revolution."

"Don't patronize me," Anatole yelled. "It was a damn fine revolution, and we haven't heard the end of it yet."

I looked at him coldly. "Would you like to hear about the Poor People's March?"

He got up from the table and stomped away, leaving me to pay the check.

HOW TO HANDLE DE GAULLE

My friend Zimmerman is a wise man, and when he speaks, I listen. One day Zimmerman said the United States was approaching the De Gaulle problem from the wrong direction.

"What exactly do you mean by that?" I asked him.

"Well, every time De Gaulle makes a statement or holds a press conference, we immediately react in rage and disbelief."

"As well we might," I said.

"But this is exactly what De Gaulle wants everybody to do. He gets his kicks out of getting everybody mad at him. The madder we get, the better he likes it. Don't you understand? De Gaulle is devoting his last years to bugging everyone, and the more we show how upset we are, the happier we make him."

"That I can believe," I said. "But what is the solution, Zimmerman?"

"We must *not* show that De Gaulle is getting under our

skin. We must make believe that everything he advocates makes sense and is in our interest as well as his."

"But how?"

"Let us suppose at his press conference De Gaulle says that Quebec should be free and no longer a part of Canada. The United States should immediately announce that not only is this a brilliant idea, but our military future depends on an autonomous Quebec. As soon as De Gaulle hears our reaction, he will drop his Free Quebec campaign and announce that Quebec must *never* be separated from the Canadian Federation."

"I could see him doing it," I said.

Zimmerman continued. "Now let us take the Common Market problem. We know De Gaulle is against Great Britain's becoming a member because he thinks we want the British in.

"The thing we must do is send word to De Gaulle, through a neutral power, that the greatest fear of the United States is that France will permit the British to become part of the European Community. We should urge De Gaulle at all costs to use his good offices to keep the British out. We might even send over Vice President Agnew to plead with him to make it impossible for the British ever to join."

"When De Gaulle hears this, he will immediately make the British a partner behind our backs," I said excitedly.

"You catch on fast," Zimmerman said. "Another thing, De Gaulle keeps making attacks on the dollar, forcing us to use up our gold reserves. Suppose we passed the word to Swiss bankers that the United States is short of dollars and we're pretending we have a gold shortage so France will sell us her dollars."

"De Gaulle will be furious and use his gold to start buying back American dollars," I cried.

"Exactly. Now we come to NATO. At the Secretary of Defense's next press conference, he should say that the Joint Chiefs of Staff have concluded that France has no strategic value in the defense of Europe, and it is to our advantage, militarily and economically, that she no longer be part of NATO."

"I'd like to see De Gaulle's face when he reads that."

"Our policy should be that no matter what DeGaulle says, we must never let on that we've lost our cool. We should praise him as a superb statesman, a magnificent soldier, and the greatest leader of our times."

"In other words, kill him with kindness," I said.

"Yes. I honestly believe that if we kept up this approach for a year, De Gaulle would lose interest in his role in the world and fade away."

"It's a cruel thing we're plotting, Zimmerman, but I think it's worth a try."

THE FRENCH AGAINST THEMSELVES

PARIS—It is a fact that France is suffering through its worst tourist season in years. Not only is this affecting the French economically, but it is also having an unbearable effect on them psychologically.

My friend Gaston explained why.

"You see, *mon cher ami*," Gaston said, "the tourist has always played a role in France far greater than he has in any other European country. It was not just a financial question—though heaven knows we were always happy to cash a traveler's check—but rather that the French could blame the tourist for everything that went wrong in France."

"I don't understand," I said.

"Well, you remember, yourself, for years after the war that every time something bad happened in France, it was the tourists' fault. If prices went up, it was because of tourists. If you couldn't get a table at a café, it was because the tourists had taken all the tables. If there were traffic jams, the French would blame the tourist buses. Every Frenchman delighted in telling an atrocity story about a tourist. It gave him a warm feeling."

"I remember it well," I said. "Even as an American living in France, I blamed the tourist for all my problems."

"It was France against the tourists—the French against the world!"

"Those were wonderful days," I said.

Gaston continued, "We all played our part. Do you know once I wrote on the pavement in front of Maxim's restaurant 'U.S. Go Home'?"

"It was the thing to do," I told Gaston. "When prices were low, the Americans didn't care."

"But, alas," said Gaston sadly, "a few years ago the tourist traffic became less and less. By last year it was no more than a trickle. This year it stopped altogether."

"Why, Gaston, why?"

"It was De Gaulle's fault. He talked so much about the grandeur of France that no tourist thought he was worthy enough to visit the country."

"Of course," I said. "Tourists have terrible inferiority complexes to start with, and it took someone like De Gaulle to scare the hell out of them."

"Exactly. No foreigners could live up to De Gaulle's image of France, so they decided to go to Spain and Italy instead."

"Italy was always stronger on souvenirs than it was on grandeur."

"But what De Gaulle didn't realize when he scared the tourists away," Gaston said, "was that the French were left without a scapegoat for all their troubles. Prices still went up, there were still traffic jams, and you still couldn't get a table at a café. For the first time since the war, the French realized that it wasn't the tourists who were to blame for all their woes; it was themselves."

"What a terrible realization," I said.

"It was more than most French could take."

"What did they do?" I asked.

"They took to the barricades."

"You mean all the troubles in France have come because there were no tourists in France?"

"Naturally," Gaston said. "You don't think the French would fight one another if there were any foreigners around?"

AN AMERICAN TOURIST IN FRANCE

PARIS—One of the rarest species in France these days is an American tourist. No one can remember the last time the French saw one, so I caused a sensation when I arrived in the French capital.

As soon as I checked in at the Hotel George V, I noticed that things had changed for Americans in the last few years. First, the concierge broke into tears; then the doorman ran to tell the bartender; the bartender called up the chef; the chef told the waiter. Everyone came out to see if an American had really checked into the hotel.

They stood around in a circle. *"C'est formidable,"* said the chef. "It is an American. I would know one any-where."

The young page stared as if I were a man from Mars.

The bartender said to him, "This was before your time, son, but once Paris was filled with thousands and thou-sands of people just like this."

"It's true," the waiter said. "They were everywhere. You could see them at the sidewalk cafés, in the shops, at the Folies Bergère, and the Lido. At one time there were so many of them there weren't enough hotel rooms to take care of them."

The page looked as if the waiter were putting him on.

The concierge said, "He is not lying, son. You couldn't get a taxi because of the Americans. You couldn't get into a restaurant or a nightclub. They had money to burn."

The doorman wiped his eyes as the memories came back. "There were so many of them we took them for granted."

The bartender shook his head. "They always wanted their martinis very dry."

The waiter said, "They always talked pidgin English, thinking you would understand them."

The chef said, "I never saw one without a camera."

"I never saw one without traveler's checks."

"They could never keep the French money straight."

"They made terrible jokes about French women."

"But they had hearts of gold."

The manager finally broke it up. By this time the word was out that an American tourist was actually in the country, and the press started to arrive.

The lobby was jammed with newspapermen and cameramen fighting to get near me.

They were shouting questions, such as: "Why did you come? Was your plane forced down by bad weather?"

"Are you really an American tourist, or do you work for the CIA?"

"Who paid you to come to France?"

"As the first American tourist to come to France, will you grant President de Gaulle an audience?"

While the press conference was going on, the police

arrived. The lieutenant came up and saluted. "The Minister of the Interior has ordered us to protect you while you are here. As the only American tourist in the country, you have been declared a national monument."

I couldn't help being touched.

The last thing I heard was that they want me to ride in the lead car in the parade down the Champs Élysées on the fourteenth of July. I guess I'll do it, for no other reason than to keep the memory of the American tourist alive.

NO BLOOD, NO SWEAT

The only bright spot in the news recently has been what has happened in Anguilla. In one of the most amazing reversals in modern military history, tiny, helpless, and, up to now, ineffectual Great Britain defeated the powerful forces of Anguilla and conquered this impregnable island fortress.

Little Britain, playing the role of David, smote the Anguillan Goliath, to the surprise of the experts and the delight of those who are constantly rooting for the underdog.

"No one thought the British could do it," said a London correspondent at the national press club, where everyone was buying drinks. "But I believe this proves once and for all Her Majesty's government can no longer be considered a paper tiger."

The bar rang with cheers. "The Anguillans bit off more than they could chew," someone shouted.

What everyone wanted to know was how the lightly armed British paratroopers and marines managed to break through the heavy Anguillan defenses, which consisted of 1 Napoleonic cannon, 12 shotguns, 3 Ford trucks, and 2,000 sheep.

"The Anguillans were overconfident," the British correspondent told us. "They thought our troops were afraid of their sheep. But we used their overconfidence to our advantage. We pulled our frigates up, and when the sheep saw them, they scattered. The sheepherders tried to rally the herds, but by this time the sheep were so disorganized they couldn't possibly put up any defense.

"It proves again that a small, tight-knit, well-trained

force of paratroopers and marines can overwhelm a much larger force of sheep if they are determined to do the job."

This was the first military defeat for Anguilla in its history, and there is great soul-searching going on now among the Anguillan armed forces, which consist of three constables, six deputies, and three Red Cross nurses. There will probably be a shake-up in the Anguillan military within the next month.

Anguilla watchers in Washington felt that the consequences of the British invasion would be felt throughout the world.

"Anguilla can no longer be considered a major power," a State Department man at the bar said.

"We have to readjust our thinking vis-à-vis their military potential. If a little country like Great Britain can defeat them, with all the hardware the Anguillans had at their disposal, then we'll have to figure out some other way of defending the Caribbean."

The London correspondent said, "We have always insisted that we could take Anguilla any time we wanted to, but everyone laughed at us. I don't imagine they're laughing anymore. The world must know by now that we just won't allow anyone to trifle with the Empire."

He went on to say that the doves in Britain had argued against the invasion, not because it was immoral, but because they didn't think the British military could do the job. But the hawks had argued that with a surprise attack they could overwhelm the Anguillans before they could get their pitchforks out of their barns. The hawks, it turned out, were right.

"Now that you've brought Anguilla to her knees," an American correspondent said, "what do you plan to do next?"

"We are a peace-loving people," the London correspondent replied. "We intervened in Anguilla only when our interests were threatened. But I think this will serve as a warning that aggression will not go unpunished in any part of the globe."

A member of the English-speaking Union raised his glass. "Today Anguilla—tomorrow the world."

6

The Computer
That Failed

THE GREAT CHART GAP

Whenever the Defense Department has to convince our lawmakers that the vital interests of the United States are in danger, they resort to elaborate displays of charts. The development, stockpiling, and delivery of charts make up one of the most critical activities the Pentagon is involved in.

Through a close friend in the Pentagon, I was permitted to visit a top-secret Defense Department Chart Testing Center, where all charts are tested before they are sent up to Capitol Hill.

The general in charge of the center said, "We've been working day and night on charts for the ABM Congressional hearings. It's probably the biggest job we've had, but one misfired chart, and the whole system could go up in smoke."

"Is this why the center is located so far from population centers?"

"Exactly. We don't want the taxpayers to know what we're doing. Also we have to watch security. The Senate Foreign Relations Committee has built a chart system of its own. We believe our charts are still more reliable than theirs, but we have to be ready with a second-strike capability in case they launch a damaging first-strike chart offensive."

"How did the charts the Senate Foreign Relations subcommittee unveiled at the ABM hearings last week differ from yours?"

The general smiled. "They were very primitive—what we could call first-generation charts. You probably noticed their charts were so large that General Gore was unable to reach the top of them with his pointer. Now we've been in the chart business a lot longer than the Senate, so we've managed to take advantage of the great strides in miniaturization, and our smaller charts can be launched from any easel with the same impact as their large ones. We can launch four charts to their one, or, if you want to put it another way, one Pentagon chart represents an overkill of thirteen Senate charts."

"What are those men doing over there?"

"They're training for chart turning."

"I beg your pardon?"

"The military has its own chart turners, who have to know when to turn a chart to the exact second. If you turn a chart too early, you lose the impact of it, and if you turn it too late, your audience could get bored."

"It must require a great deal of skill," I said.

"All of our chart turners have been to the National War College and have been personally interviewed by Admiral Rickover. If you recall, a few weeks ago when Senator Gore's subcommittee produced its charts against the ABM system, they had to press their chief counsel and his assistant into service as chart turners. It was a disaster."

"What is that building over there with the machine guns on it and all the MP's around it?"

"That's where we're developing a new top-secret automatic chart-turning machine. Once it is deployed, no Senate committee will dare attack a Defense Department budget."

"But won't this spiral the chart race and force the subcommittee to develop its own automatic chart turner?"

The general said, "When the security of the Pentagon is at stake, we are not interested in chart parity."

HE THOUGHT UP THE DOMINO THEORY

One of the most discussed political theories of our time is the so-called domino theory which is used to justify most of the reasons why we are in Vietnam. The domino theory is based on the premise that countries in Southeast Asia are like so many dominoes, and if one falls, the next one will fall until every country out there is down and taken over by godless Communism.

While there has been a great deal of talk about the domino theory, very little attention has been paid to the man who originally thought it up, and I decided it was time somebody talked to him.

His name, it turns out, is Sam Domino, and he lives in

Forest Hills, New York, where I found him on a recent Sunday afternoon playing gin rummy.

When I expressed surprise at this, he explained, "Dominoes bore me."

"Mr. Domino, your domino theory is the touchstone of our American military and diplomatic thrust in Southeast Asia. Could you explain how you thought it up?"

"Well, one evening we were having a buffet, and there were about twenty people lined up with plates waiting for some chicken cacciatore when my uncle, who was first in line, slipped and fell backward. He knocked over my aunt standing in back of him, and she in turn knocked over my cousin, who knocked over my son, and so on until all twenty people were on the floor. It suddenly occurred to me that if this could happen to people, it could happen to countries.

"So what did you do?"

"I wrote a letter to John Foster Dulles, who was then our Secretary of State."

"But who named it the domino theory?"

"My wife. She said when she read the letter, 'Sam, put your name on it or they won't give you any credit.' At first I was reluctant to do so, but then I figured I had nothing to lose, so I specifically said that if they used any part of my letter, they'd have to mention me as the author of the theory.

"Much to my surprise, Dulles answered the letter. He said that up until I had written, the State Department had been fooling around with brinkmanship, which had been advocated by a man named Brinkman, who lived in Bethesda, Maryland. Dulles felt that the domino theory was a new approach to the cold war, and he thanked me personally for bringing it to his attention."

"How did he know it would work?"

"He lined up twenty State Department employees in the cafeteria and tried the same experiment. When the first one in line fell, the others fell behind him. This was proof enough as far as he was concerned."

"And so the domino theory was then practically applied to the countries in Southeast Asia?"

"Yup. From then through the Kennedy and Johnson administrations our whole commitment in that part of the world was based on my theory. If it hadn't been for my wife, no one would have ever heard of me."

"You must be very proud."

"I am, but I'm starting to get a little worried."

"What is that?"

"The other night I had another party, and again my uncle was first in line and again he fell; but this time everyone was braced for it and no one else fell. It shot my domino theory to hell."

"You'd better get off a letter to the Secretary of State right away."

"My wife said I'd better forget it. I've caused enough trouble already."

THE COMPUTER THAT FAILED

When the Vietnam War was raging at its fiercest, David Brinkley reported that a scientist had programmed all the pertinent military information about the United States and North Vietnam and fed it into a computer, raising the question: When will the war be won and which side will win?

The computer answered that the United States had won the war two years ago.

I decided to go see the computer to find out what went wrong.

The computer seemed very annoyed when I fed it the question. It replied on the tape, "Nobody's perfect."

"I'm not trying to criticize you, sir, but it does seem that the results do not gibe with the facts."

"There are a lot of unpredictable factors in this that I can't be responsible for. All I was doing was computing relative strengths of the United States and North Vietnam military, enemy troop morale factors based on CIA reports, information gleaned from defectors, pacification results, General Westmoreland's optimism, and the high esteem the South Vietnamese people hold for their government. If you had digested all these facts, you would have come up with the same answer."

"Then you didn't include any information out of Hanoi?"

"Why should I? The State Department told me not to believe anything Hanoi says."

"Did you take into consideration the American bombing of North Vietnam?"

"Of course I did. Why else would I have said the United States had won? Everyone knows that if you drop a certain ratio of bombs on a given country during a given time, that country has to surrender."

"But they didn't."

"It's not my fault those people don't think like a computer."

"I'm not criticizing you. I'm just trying to find out where you made your mistakes. How do you explain the fact that despite the fighting and the victories the Americans have amassed over there, the Vietcong were able to launch a drive on the cities?"

The computer shuddered. "That was not my error. I just accepted the body counts of the last five years, ran them through, and, on the basis of my figures, came to the conclusion that every Vietcong was either dead or had defected. As a computer, I can't very well go around counting bodies myself."

"That's true. Now I understand one of the reasons you came to your decision was based on captured enemy documents. How did you err there?"

"Somebody captured the wrong enemy documents. Look, I'm just a machine. You can't lay all the blame at my feet."

"Yes, but there are thousands of computers like you, and if every one of them comes up with the wrong answers, we could be in a mess, couldn't we?"

"Only if there is a credibility gap somewhere along the line."

"Have you made allowances for that?"

"I'm a loyal American computer, and if I made allowances for a credibility gap, I'd only be giving aid and comfort to the enemy."

"Well, since you goofed so badly on the last go-round when do you think the war will be over now?"

"That's not up to me. That's up to Hanoi."

"OVER THERE, OVER THERE"

One of the troubles with the Vietnam War is that no one has been able to write a war song to go with it. Everyone knows you can't have a really good war without a socko song that people can sing and whistle back in the United States.

For four years, Tin Pan Alley has been working day and night on a war song, without success. Not long ago I looked in on two friends of mine, Al and Leo, who, despite the efforts at peace talks, were still determined to come up with a war song this country could be proud of.

When I walked in, Al was singing, "It's a long way to the Mekong Delta/It's a long way to go./Keep your eye out for the Vietcong/They're a sneaky bunch, you know."

Al tore up the manuscript in disgust. "I just can't seem to get it."

Leo said, "I don't know what's the matter with us. How do you like this one: 'Pack up your napalm in your old kit bag/And smile, smile, smile!'?"

"It doesn't send me," I had to admit.

"The trouble with this damn war," Al said, "is that it's got too many sociological aspects. It's so complicated."

"That's right," Leo agreed. "Have you ever tried to write lyrics about a pacification program? I tell you, it's downright discouraging. Do you know at one time we were the best war-song writers in the business?"

"We wrote 'Shut Your Trap, You Dirty Jap, or Uncle Sam Will Shut It for You' in twelve minutes in 1942," Al said.

"And don't forget the 'Adolf Hitler Polka'," Leo added.

"Those were the good old days," Al said, "when you could really get your teeth into the enemy. We had yellow-belly Nips and goose-stepping Krauts."

"And fat-lipped Mussolini hanging over the balcony," Leo said.

"And Tokyo Rose and Lord Haw-Haw and fat-faced Göring, and shorty Goebbels. Man, they were enemies."

"Look what we have now," Leo said. "Ho Chi Minh looks like a starving Santa Claus, and no one in North Vietnam weighs more than eighty-seven pounds."

"It could be a problem," I had to admit to the boys.

"Washington has begged us for four years to write something. They said the war would never catch on unless people were singing about it. And they were right," Leo said.

Al said, "We're not copping a plea, but this war just

doesn't have the old drive, the old caissons, the old Patton, the old MacArthur, the ole 'Praise the Lord and Pass the Ammunition' feeling."

Leo said, "The fun's gone out of war-song writing."

I said, "I can't believe it, men. You can't tell me that after all these years you guys can't come up with an inspirational song about the Vietnam War. Surely you can come up with something that would make this country believe we're doing the right thing."

Al sat down at the piano and started to sing: "Over there/Over there/Send the word/Send the word/To beware. Without negotiation/There'll be escalation/And we won't stop bombing till it's over, over there."

Leo said, "It's no 'Let's Remember Pearl Harbor.' "

"It isn't even 'Roll Me Over in the Clover'," I said.

Al continued singing: "We'll be over/We're coming over/And we won't come back until, until it's been clearly established that the South Vietnamese will be free to decide their own destinies under the full Geneva Agreements and aggression from the North will be discontinued and the bases in Cambodia and Laos will be dismantled, so help us God."

"It's got a good feeling to it," I told Al, "but it doesn't rhyme."

WHY THE VIETCONG FAILED

One of the many discussions still raging in the nation's capital is whether the Vietcong did or did not get into the American Embassy in Saigon. The official government position is that they did not.

One of our public servants told me, "You newspaper people went overboard on the story. The truth is that although the Vietcong penetrated the embassy grounds, they never did get into the chancery. Since they did not achieve their objective, we consider this one of the worst defeats the Communists have ever suffered in the downtown district of Saigon."

"That may be true," I said, "but there are some people who feel that penetration of the embassy grounds by the Vietcong gave the American effort in Vietnam a black eye."

"Balderdash," my friend said. "The question was never

in doubt. Even if the Vietcong had captured the embassy, we weren't worried."

"You weren't?"

"Of course not. Everyone knows the Vietcong don't know how to operate an American Embassy."

I guess I must have looked stunned.

He continued: "Let us suppose the worst happened and the Vietcong did get into the embassy. Do you think they have any notion of how to issue visas or passports or handle the fantastic amount of paperwork that an embassy of this size requires?"

"Well, they aren't trained for it," I had to admit.

"Of course they're not. Our intelligence showed that not one of the nineteen Vietcong who invaded the embassy grounds had any foreign service experience at all."

"Then why would the Vietcong try to take over the American Embassy?"

"Because they're smug, and it's this smugness that's going to defeat them in the long run. They think they can just walk into one of our embassies and have it running smoothly in six hours. Well, they found out they couldn't. It wasn't just a case of not knowing how to issue passports. Do you know not one of those guerrillas was capable of writing a report to Washington that anyone could have understood?"

"I forgot about writing reports to Washington."

"It's obvious they did, too, or they would have sent a much higher caliber man. Any idiot knows that one of the most important functions of an American Embassy is to cable back clear, precise, reliable reports on the conditions of the country. In the case of Vietnam, they would have had to supply reports on the pacification program, the military assistance program, the AID program, as well as transmit daily body counts to the White House. How they ever expected to do these reports with only nineteen men, I'll never know."

"Maybe they were going to bring in more people after they captured the embassy," I suggested.

"It isn't just a question of paperwork and reports," my friend continued. "An American Embassy has to keep up relations with the government, as well as other embassies. Do you think anybody in a prominent position in Saigon would come to an American Embassy reception if he knew it were being catered by the Vietcong?"

"Socially, they'd be cut dead," I agreed.

"It wouldn't have taken more than a week before the Vietcong realized the disastrous mistake they had made," my source said. "Bogged down in paperwork, besieged by requests from Washington for optimistic reports on how the war was going, faced with the prospect of dealing with President Thieu and Marshal Ky, it would have just been a matter of time before the Communists came to us on their hands and knees and begged us to take back the American Embassy."

"Would you?"

"Only if they indicated by some sign or action that they really wanted peace in South Vietnam."

CUSTER'S LAST PRESS CONFERENCE

LITTLE BIGHORN, Dakota, June 27, 1876—General George Armstrong Custer said today in an exclusive interview with this correspondent that the Battle of Little Bighorn had just turned the corner and he could now see the light at the end of the tunnel.

"We have the Sioux on the run," General Custer told me. "Of course, we still have some cleaning up to do, but the redskins are hurting badly, and it will only be a matter of time before they give in."

"That's good news, General. Of course, there are people who are skeptical about the military briefings on this war, and they question if we're getting the entire truth as to what is really happening here."

"I just would like to refer you to these latest body counts. The Sioux lost five thousand men to our one hundred. They can't hope to keep up this attrition much longer. We know for a fact Sioux morale is low, and they are ready to throw in the towel."

"Well, if they're hurting so badly, General Custer, how do you explain this massive attack?"

"It's a desperation move on the part of Sitting Bull and his last death rattle. I have here captured documents which show that this is Phase Two of Sitting Bull's plan to wrest the Black Hills from the Americans. All he's going for is a psychological victory, but the truth is that we expected this all the time and we're not surprised by it."

"What about the fact that nineteen Indians managed to penetrate your headquarters? Doesn't that look bad?"

"We knew all along they planned to penetrate my headquarters at the Indian Lunar New Year. The fact that we repulsed them after they held on for only six hours is another example of how badly the Sioux are fighting. Besides, they never did get into the sleeping quarters of my tent, so I don't really think they should be credited with penetrating my headquarters."

"You seem to be surrounded at the moment, General."

"Obviously the enemy plans have gone afoul," General Custer said. "The Sioux are hoping to win a big victory so they'll be able to have something to talk about at the conference table. Look at this latest body count. We've just killed three thousand more Indians and lost fifty of our men."

"Then, according to my figuring, General, you have only fifty men left."

"Exactly. They can't keep up this pressure much longer. The truth of the matter is that their hit-and-run guerrilla tactics haven't worked, so they're now resorting to mass attacks against our positions. Thanks to our interdiction of their supply lines, they are short not only of bows and arrows, but gunpowder as well."

An aide came in and handed General Custer a sheet of paper. "I knew it," the general said. "The latest body count shows they've lost two thousand more Injuns in the last hour. They should be suing for peace at any time."

"How many did we lose, General?"

"Our losses were light. We only lost forty-five men."

"But, General, that means you have only five men left, including yourself."

"Look, we have to lose some men, but we're taking all precautions to keep our losses to a minimum. Besides, we can always count on the friendly Indians in these hills to turn against the Sioux for starting hostilities during the Indian Lunar New Year."

The aide staggered back in, an arrow in his chest. He handed General Custer a slip of paper and then dropped at his feet.

"Well, they just lost five hundred more. And we only lost four. It looks as if they've had it."

"But, General, that means you're the only one left."

"Boy," said the general, "would I hate to be in Sioux shoes right now."

CURING A PHOBIA

One of the things that General Curtis LeMay said at a recent press conference was that Americans seem to have a phobia about nuclear weapons. This struck home because I have to admit I've had such a phobia for some time. But only after General LeMay brought it up did I decide to do something about it. I went to see Dr. Adolph Strainedluff, a psychiatrist who specializes in nuclear weapon phobias.

"On the couch," he said. "Vat seems to be the trouble?"

"Doctor," I said staring at the ceiling, "I have this fear of nuclear weapons. I know it's silly, but to me it's very real."

"Aha, very hinterasting. Ven did you first become aware of such a phobia?"

"I think it was around the time of Hiroshima or Nagasaki, I'm not sure which. I saw these photos of all these people killed and miles and miles of rubble, and suddenly I got this thing about atomic weapons."

Dr. Strainedluff tapped a pencil against his knee. "So tell me, how does this phobia manifest itself?"

"In peculiar ways, Doctor. I get the feeling if I ever see a mushroom cloud, I'm going to die."

"Very hinterasting, very hinterasting. You know it's all in the mind, don't you?"

"Of course. That's why I came to you. I don't want to do anything stupid."

Dr. Strainedluff said, "You are a very sick man. You think that just because an atomic bomb killed a few thousand people more than twenty years ago, you are threatened. You are manifesting infantile repressed hostility toward the weapons of war. In psychiatry we call this a military-industrial inferiority complex."

"I know I'm sick. You've got to help me," I begged.

"All right. First, you haff to get over this absurd fear of nuclear bombs. You must think of them as just another weapon in our vast defensive arsenal. Ve haff bowie knives and H-bombs, and in war, one is just as good as another. You're not afraid of a knife, are you?"

"Well, I don't think about it a lot."

"So vhy should you be afraid of an H-bomb? It's another form of a knife."

"I never thought of it like that."

"Okay, so now let's look at some facts straight in the eye. In Bikini we blew up twenty bombs in an experiment. So ve thought everything vould be destroyed; that's how stupid ve were. Do you know that now after all the boom-boom, the place is flourishing and the rats are fatter than they ever vas before?"

"It's good to hear."

"The coconuts are hanging from the trees, the fish are svimming in the lagoon, and the voice of the turtle can be heard in the land. The only things that don't seem to be doing so good are the land crabs."

"I don't like land crabs," I said.

"So then you don't haff anything to vorry about."

Dr. Strainedluff started playing with the hand grenade which was attached to his watch fob. "If you're going to be a happy, normal human being," he shouted, "you're going to haff to stop with all these guilty peace feelings."

He was stomping around the room. "So get out of here vith your lousy phobias and all this stuff about being afraid to die. If you're not villing to take a little fallout for the good of the country, then go back vhere you came from!"

In spite of Dr. Strainedluff's final outburst, he did cure me of my phobia. I'm no longer afraid of nuclear weapons. Now I'm afraid of him.

PEACE SCARE NO. 30

Whenever we have a peace scare in the United States as we have been experiencing lately, I search out my dear friend, General Hurtus Dismay, formerly of the Air Force Bomber Command, who knows more about war than any living authority.

"Is peace inevitable?" I asked General Dismay, who had just returned from a three-day trip to Vietnam.

"Not necessarily. In the atomic age we must always live with the threat of peace, but I think it can be avoided."

"But how?"

"First, by not making any overtures to the enemy that might provoke them into thinking that we want peace, and, second, by ignoring any peace feelers from the other side, no matter how promising they are. When peace threatens, you must use all the military know-how you have to prevent it from becoming a reality."

"But how can you do this, General?"

"Quite simple. If the enemy lets up on the fighting, you announce they are losing the war and it is the best time to go in and clean them out once and for all. If the enemy continues fighting, you announce that the enemy has no intention of seeking peace and they must be beaten with every weapon at your disposal. The worst thing to show during a peace scare is any sign of weakness."

"What, in your opinion, is the best way to avoid all-out peace?"

"By stepping up the bombing. The more you bomb, the less chance you have of someone making a mistake that could lead to peace negotiations.

"One of the problems you have to deal with when you fight a war is the civilian-nonindustrial complex, which seems intent on provoking peace for its own selfish gains. If we left it up to the complex, there would be some kind of peace every ten years."

"Does the President of the United States realize this?"

"At the beginning President Johnson had his guard up against the peacemongers, but as time went on, he was under so much pressure from special interest groups who have more to gain from peace than war that he started giving in, against the best advice of the military. During the first four years in Vietnam, there was never any talk of peace. We prevailed because we had persuaded the President that we could win the war without peace. But then the President got cold feet and initiated the Paris peace talks, which we feel could eventually lead to a peaceful confrontation between the two sides. If both sides refused to back down, and wanted to wage peace, then I wouldn't even want to imagine the consequences."

"What can the average citizen do to avoid a peaceful settlement in Vietnam?"

"He can demand the continuation of the bombing, the invasion of North Vietnam, the pursuit of the enemy into

Laos and Cambodia, and deescalation of the war so we can win it once and for all."

"But will anybody listen?" I asked.

"Maybe not at first. If enough people raise their voices against the peace, they will have to do something about it."

"But every time I raise my voice against peace in Vietnam, I'm called a hawk," I cried.

"This is a question of conscience, and if you really believe in war as a way of settling things, you have to expect to be ridiculed and called names. History is on your side. In the age of sophisticated weaponry and nuclear hardware, peace can no longer be considered a feasible way of solving our problems."

"You've given me great strength, General," I said.

He put his hand on my shoulder. "Don't despair. Even if peace seems inevitable, somehow we'll muddle through."

HOW THEY BROKE THE NEWS TO JOHNSON

There continues to be a great deal of speculation about why Lyndon Johnson had been informed so late on the capture of the Navy intelligence ship *Pueblo*.

Many versions have been given concerning what happened during those key moments before the President was informed on the *Pueblo*'s fate.

Here is one I heard, though I, of course, cannot verify every fact.

When the news hit Washington at 11 P.M., it was first passed through lower channels at the Pentagon and the State Department before it was brought to the attention of Secretary McNamara and Secretary Rusk.

McNamara called Rusk and said, "I think you'd better notify the President. This is a diplomatic problem."

"The heck it is," said the usually taciturn Dean Rusk. "That was a Navy ship, and it's Defense's problem. You'd better notify the President."

"Wait a minute, Dean," said Secretary McNamara. "I just had to tell the President about our losing four hydrogen bombs over Greenland. He's going to start thinking of me as a purveyor of bad news.

"Besides," McNamara added, "that ship wasn't on a Navy mission. It was on an intelligence mission."

"Then Dick Helms of the CIA ought to tell the President," Rusk concluded.

A call was placed to Helms, and when Secretary Rusk informed him of the situation, Helms couldn't have been more surprised.

"You'd better tell the President," Rusk said.

"I'd rather not if it's all the same to you," Helms said. "Besides, I don't have the White House telephone number. Say, I have an idea. Let's get Walt Rostow to tell him. Walt works in the White House so he's probably adept at breaking bad news to the President."

"All right," Rusk said. "I guess Walt is as good at this sort of thing as anybody."

Secretary Rusk woke Walt Rostow up and told him the news. He suggested Rostow go over to the White House immediately and tell the President. Rostow agreed and started to get dressed.

After finishing his eggs, Rostow drove over to the darkened White House. He was quite frantic about how he would break the news to the President at such an ungodly hour. Nervously he walked up the stairway to the President's bedroom.

As he got to the room, an inspiration hit him. He opened the door and got down on his hands and knees and started crawling toward the bed. When he got there he grasped the President's hand.

"That you, Lynda Bird?" the President sleepily inquired.

"No, it's Walt."

"Walt who?"

"Walt Rostow, your White House aide."

"Well, what in tarnation are you doing on your hands and knees at this hour? Eartha Kitt isn't coming to breakfast, is she?"

"No, sir, I have something else to tell you."

"What is it?" the President said.

"Do you mind if I get in bed? It's very confidential."

"Blast it, Walt, what do you want to say?"

"Well, I know you're not going to believe this . . ."

At that moment Lady Bird woke up. "What's going on, Lyndon?" she demanded.

"Nothing, Lady Bird. Walt Rostow is just trying to tell me something important."

"Whew, I had a fright there for a moment," Lady Bird said. "I was afraid Lynda Bird and Chuck had had their first fight."

WHY COULDN'T WE HAVE BEEN FISHING?

Everyone is second-guessing what we should have done or not done about the hijacking of the USS *Pueblo,* which, depending on whom you believe, had been either on the high seas or in the territorial waters of North Korea.

What everyone does agree on is that the *Pueblo* was an electronic snooper, spying on North Korea, and that the operation was pretty botched up.

I had no idea what we could have done differently until I bumped into my friend Dmitri, a Soviet Embassy employee who I'm quite sure is a spy.

Strangely enough, Dmitri seemed very upset about the *Pueblo*'s capture.

"Is making it hard on all spy ships," Dmitri said. "Because of *Pueblo*, now all spy ships are looked on with suspicion."

"But what could we have done differently?" I asked Dmitri.

"Is not my place to help Americans in espionage, but you went about spying on North Korea all wrong."

"What would you have done?"

"Fish."

"What do you mean, 'fish'?" I said angrily.

"Is well-known fact that all Soviet spy ships are fishing trawlers. They are manned by civilians dressed as fishermen. Every time they go somewhere, three civilians throw their fishing lines over side of trawler and fish. Then, if boat drifts into territorial waters, everyone is arrested for illegal fishing."

"That did happen in Alaska," I admitted.

"Is happening all the time," Dmitri said. "Suppose instead of U.S. Navy ship, the United States sent in fishing trawler. Everyone knows the fish off North Korea are running good at this time of year. So you show up off Wonsan and throw nets out. Torpedo boat comes out and yells, 'Hey, you dirty capitalistic, rotten, revisionist fisherman, stop fishing in our waters.' So your captain yells, 'Is free waters for fish. Americans need fish for to win hearts and minds of people in the free world. Drop dead, stupid torpedo boat.' "

"That's provocative," I said.

"Is only stupid fishing captain speaking—not voice of U.S. Navy. Torpedo boat gets mad and calls for fishing warden, who boards trawler and arrests captain for fishing in North Korean waters. So what do headlines read? Page forty-five it says, 'American fishing boat arrested by North Korean fishing warden.'

"Two days later, story is now on page sixty-five and says, 'American fisherman pay fine. United States promises to punish stupid captain.' Is no big incident, and the next time we get caught spying in your waters, you can get back your money. Don't you see? No one gets mad when fisherman get arrested. Is happening all the time."

"I'll have to admit you're right, Dmitri. Even I wouldn't have gotten angry if they had arrested American fishermen. After all, fishermen do have to take risks."

"Not only that," Dmitri said. "But is well-known fact even if your boat doesn't get arrested, CIA can always use fresh fish."

"Dmitri," I said, "I'm going to pass on your suggestion to the powers that be. But it's obvious you've been ordered to make this suggestion to me. Why?"

"Is true, what you say. Soviet Secret Service is having money problems. If American Secret Service looks lousy, they'll cut *our* budget. We have to make you look good, or we won't get any more rubles for our brand-new fishing trawlers."

INSTANT RESEARCH

The seismograph in Washington, D.C., showed a slight quake in the credibility gap when Undersecretary of Defense David Packard testified in front of the Senate Foreign Relations Subcommittee on Disarmament on the ABM. Asked to name a science adviser not connected with the Pentagon who had participated in a review of the missile system, Packard came up with Dr. Wolfgang K. H. Panofsky, a noted physicist from Stanford.

Unfortunately for Packard, Dr. Panofsky denied he had

participated in any review of the Safeguard system and said he was opposed to it. He also said that his only encounter with Packard was an accidental meeting at the airport in San Francisco, where the men talked informally about different defense systems while waiting for their planes.

I was very curious about the Pentagon's new method of talking to scientists, and I was fortunate to run into a friend who happens to be an Assistant Secretary of Defense. He was standing next to the insurance counter at New York's LaGuardia Field.

"Where are you going?" I asked him.

"I'm not going anywhere," he said. "I'm stationed here working on a research project."

"What do you mean?"

"We're interviewing scientists at airports on the ABM."

"Why at the airports?" I asked.

"None of them wants to come to Washington, so we have to catch them on the run. Look, there's Professor Bezilsky of Harvard University." He stopped the professor.

"Dr. Bezilsky," he said, "my name's Carnaby of the Defense Department, and I was wondering if you could give me your opinion of the ultrahigh frequencies in radar simulation vis-à-vis the ABM."

Professor Bezilsky looked annoyed. "I haf to catch my plane."

"It will only take a minute, sir."

"Please, this is not the place to go into ultrahigh frequencies in radio simulation," Bezilsky said, trying to move on.

"Professor, are you for it or against it?"

"Vill you let me catch my plane, *Dummkopf?*"

Bezilsky pushed Carnaby aside and rushed off with his bag.

Carnaby said, "Well, he's for it."

"How did you figure that?" I asked him.

"Our orders are that if a scientist doesn't come out specifically and say he's against the ABM, then he must be for it." Carnaby wrote something in his notebook. "I have four scientists for the ABM and one against."

"That's marvelous," I said in admiration. "All you have to do is wait by the New York to Boston shuttle and you catch the whole MIT, Harvard, and Tufts Scientific Establishment."

"Right. It's foolproof because we could never get to talk to this many scientists in Washington. Oh, my goodness, look who's over there—it's Dr. Heinrich Spitzelbaron, who discovered manifold pressure under glass. Dr. Spitzelbaron, Dr. Spitzelbaron, would you care to participate in an instant seminar we're holding here on the ABM system?"

"No, but I'd like to buy some flight insurance. I'm scared to death of flying."

"But what about the threat of the Soviet Multiple Weapon Launchers and their first-strike superiority?"

"If I could just get to Cleveland safely, I'd be grateful."

"Doctor, could I ask you about the Chinese first generation of nuclear weapons?"

"I usually get drunk when I fly," Dr. Spitzelbaron said. "I know it's stupid, but I'm afraid of heights."

After he bought his insurance and left, I asked Carnaby, "Is he pro or con?"

"If I had to testify in front of a Senate committee, I'd say he was pro—but with a few reservations."

REARMAMENT CONFERENCE

A short time ago Israel and Jordan had a shoot-out. After it was over, Israeli political circles were quoted as saying they feared that the decision of the United States to supply Jordan with arms would upset the armament balance in the Middle East. At the same time, Israel would not make any protest since it preferred the Jordanians' getting arms from Washington instead of from the Soviet Union, which is hostile to Israel.

It may be just grabbing at a straw, but perhaps the solution for peace may be that instead of nations holding "disarmament" conferences, they could meet to discuss "rearmament." If they could agree on how much they were going to rearm, some of the suspicion about disarmament could disappear.

Let us suppose that Jordan and Israel met in Geneva to discuss the problem.

"We're getting fifty F-100's from the United States," the Jordanians say.

"That's perfectly all right with us," the Israelis reply. "We're getting fifty American F-5's. They're much faster and can also carry rockets."

"Is that so? Maybe we should get F-5's as well."

"Well, we don't want to tell you how to run your defense, but you're crazy to take the F-100's if you can get the F-5's," the Israelis say.

"That's good of you to warn us. By the way, our intelligence reports indicate that those new American tanks you bought won't stand up against the antitank guns the Americans gave us."

"No kidding? Where are the weaknesses?" the Israelis ask.

"In the turret. Maybe you could add some armor in the turret to compensate for the deficiency."

"I think we could. Oh, by the way, we read in the newspapers that the Jordanians are buying some 105 artillery guns. They're pretty expensive, you know."

"You don't think we should buy them?"

"Well, we looked over your military budget, and you would be much better off investing your money in mortars. There is a new AK mortar we purchased, and we're quite satisfied with it."

"Of course, why didn't we think of mortars?" the Jordanians say. "Do you have any dope on antiaircraft missiles?"

"Be careful about which missile you select. The Americans have sold us an antimissile-missile system that's pretty good, and you'll just be throwing your dough away on an antiaircraft missile."

"That's really a valuable piece of information. Why are you being so helpful?"

"Well, we'd rather you get your stuff from the United States. If you're dissatisfied with what you get from the Americans, you might turn to the Soviet Union for help."

"By the way," the Jordanians say, "one of our biggest items is the cost of shipping the hardware to Jordan. Sometimes when Israel doesn't have a full shipload, perhaps we could put some of it on your ships. After all, it's going to *practically* the same place. If we could pool our shipping expenses, we'd have more money to spend on the M-16 rifle."

"Hold off on the M-16 rifle. There are still bugs in it," the Israelis say. "In spite of what they say, it still jams."

"I don't know if this makes sense or not," the Jordanian says, "but if your Minister of Defense and our Minister of Defense could fly over to Washington together, then they could lay out their needs and there would be coordination on what we bought."

"I'll bring it up with General Dayan. It could save us a lot of trouble. The beauty of the arrangement is if one or the other of us ran out of spare parts for the American equipment, we could borrow it from the other."

THE PUBLIC'S RIGHT TO KNOW

My friend Mulligan was in a stew. "I'm getting sick of all this 'public's right to know' business."

"What are you talking about?" I asked him

"I've been watching the ABM hearings for two days, and I'll be damned if I know what they're talking about."

"But, Mulligan, these things should be thrashed out in the open. We have a big stake in the ABM, and if we don't know the pros and cons of the system, we all could be in a jam."

"Is that so?" Mulligan said. "It so happens I was much happier not knowing about the ABM. I was minding my own business. I wasn't aware of the Soviets' first-strike peril, I couldn't have cared less about our second-strike deterrent capability, and I didn't even know there was a generation gap in our missiles."

"A generation gap in our missiles?" I said in astonishment.

"Sure. Don't you realize that our first-generation missiles are being threatened by the Soviets' second-generation missiles, which will soon be replaced by more sophisticated third-generation missiles?"

"I certainly didn't."

"I wish I didn't know, either. I suppose you're also unaware that the Soviets' SS-Nine ICBM's are now in full production and will eventually have multiple nuclear warheads that could destroy five or six cities in the United States at the same time. How would you like to go to sleep with that knowledge every night?"

"I'd hate to dream about it."

"What's going on in this country anyway?" Mulligan said. "In the days gone by, before the public had a right to know, we had guys to do our worrying for us.

"It was their job to stew about someone blowing up the world. Now they tell us everything, and we're supposed to figure out what they're talking about. It's like a brain surgeon showing you twenty different instruments and asking you which one you want him to use for the operation."

"You're overwrought, Mulligan. The reason that they want you informed on matters pertaining to nuclear defense is that the people charged with safeguarding our country don't want to make mistakes. They feel if the public is aware of the danger, then they'll get the support so necessary to implement the decisions."

"Big deal. What am I supposed to do—pick up the phone and say, 'Hey, Secretary Laird, if I were you, I wouldn't worry about the Soviet first-strike peril. Come up with a more feasible Multiple Independently Targetable Reentry Vehicle that won't cost too much and I'll put in a good word for you with the Daughters of the American Revolution'?"

"Now you're not being reasonable," I admonished Mulligan.

"Reasonable? We don't even know if the Minuteman ICBM's will work, so how the hell are we supposed to know if the ABM's work? Suppose the ABM system is protecting missiles that can't get off the ground?"

"You don't have all the facts at your command to make that judgment," I said.

"You're damn right I don't," said Mulligan. "So I don't want to know any facts at all. You have to be a physicist to understand the questions, much less the answers, at the televised hearings. I say if they're going to mess around, let them do it in private. I really don't have any interest in how many more years we have before the Chinese can blow us up."

"You're being unfair to our leaders. All they're trying to do is share their awesome responsibility with you."

"If I wanted that awesome responsibility, I would have run for President or asked Mr. Nixon to make me Secretary of Defense," Mulligan said. "I'll make a deal with the administration. I'll worry about the sportswear business if they don't bug me with their problems about the ABM."

"You don't have the nuclear-team spirit, Mulligan. Aren't you at least interested in the missiles we're building for peace?"

Mulligan shook his head. "If you've seen one military-industrial complex, you've seen 'em all."

7

Up Against The Wall

BACK TO THE BACK OF THE BUS

I'm not saying it happened—but it could have.

A black man dressed in an African caftan walked into a bus station coffee shop and sat down next to a white man wearing a white sheet and hood with the letters KKK written on the front.

"I beg your pardon," said the white man. "What is that outfit you're wearing?"

"I'm a black militant, honky."

"What a coincidence," the other man said. "I'm a *white* militant. Where are you going?"

"I'm going to a demonstration to demand all-black housing for college students in black dormitories."

"That's wonderful," said the KKK man. "We've been saying for years that the blacks should live by themselves."

"You have?"

"Of course. You should have your own restaurants, your own hotels, your own movie theaters, and your own place on trains."

"You putting me on?"

"I am not. You can look it up if you want to. We've worked, it seems forever, to see that the black people didn't have anything to do with the white people. For your benefit, of course."

"Hey, that's crazy. You white cats are working for the same thing we are. How do you feel about integrating?"

"We're absolutely against it. If it weren't for the Supreme Court, you people would have all the black things you wanted. They forced you to mix with the white man."

"The Supreme Court has no right to tell us to mix with honkies."

"They certainly don't. You should be segregated if that's what you want. We think you should have your own drinking fountains, too."

"That's for sure. Don't want to drink from no fountain a white's drunk out of."

"I'd feel the same way if I were you. Do you know our organization advocates black and white washrooms in railroad stations and bus terminals?"

"I didn't know there were any honkies thought that."

"You better believe it. We're on your side. Why, up until a few years ago we insisted on separate education for the races—black in black shools, white in white schools."

"Man, that's what my demonstration's all about."

"And listen to this. We felt so strongly about the black man living in his own black neighborhood that when some Uncle Tom moved into a white neighborhood, we burned a cross on his lawn."

"Good for you," the black man said. "Black people want to move in white neighborhoods are nothing more than plantation slaves."

"I've never said this to a black man before, but I like the way you think."

"Thanks, honky. You know I usually won't talk to a white man. But you're different. You're working for the same things we're working for."

"Of course we are. Someday, if you're successful and we're successful, we won't even have to eat together in this restaurant. There will be a section for you and a section for us."

"Beautiful. I can't wait for that day."

"Well, we better get on the bus."

"Yeah. I wonder where I should sit."

"Why don't you sit in the back? It's much more comfortable there."

THE SLEEP-IN

FORT LAUDERDALE, Florida—Beatle John Lennon and his bride, Yoko Ono, told newsmen that they would stay in bed in their Amsterdam hotel for seven days and seven nights during their honeymoon to protest violence in the world.

This sleep-in, if it catches on, could turn out to be the most popular type of protest ever thought up by the peace movement, and the authorities are not too sure yet how to handle it.

Since anything the Beatles do seems to be adopted, it's quite possible that Mr. and Mrs. Lennon's tactics will soon become part of the student nonviolent scene.

I was lucky to interview students at Fort Lauderdale who were on Easter vacation to get their reaction.

One said, "I wish we had known about it in Chicago. We would have had a lot less casualties."

But his friend disagreed. "Knowing the Chicago cops, they would have probably come into our rooms and busted our beds."

A third student seemed doubtful that Lennon's tactic was practical. "You can't get that kind of protest on television, except maybe on educational TV. And if you don't get on television, there doesn't seem to be any sense in protesting."

This opinion was shared by a University of North Carolina sophomore. "I could sleep in a park for seven days and seven nights, but I don't think it would work if I had to stay indoors. Like I mean, man, the fun of the protest is to be with your friends. It's no kick holding up a picket sign if nobody is going to see it."

But a co-ed from Swarthmore disagreed. "If all the students disappeared for seven days and seven nights, we'd have this country really uptight. They would have no idea what was happening."

An MIT engineering major shook his head. "I'd be for a sleep-in only if Secretary of HEW Finch assured me I would not lose my federal aid for doing it. They're going to have to put out some guidelines before I get into bed."

"They can't take your federal aid away from you for sleeping," a Harvard law student said, "as long as you do it peacefully."

"Sure," the MIT student said, "that's what they tell you now, but who's going to say if you were sleeping peacefully or not? Suppose you have a restless night?"

An Oberlin music major said, "That shouldn't be our concern. If sleeping is going to make this country wake up to the fact that we want peace, then I say we should sleep."

Her girlfriend said, "After a week in Fort Lauderdale I'll need seven days and seven nights of sleep, even if it isn't for peace."

"I think," said an Amherst student, "we should wait and

see. After all, the only reason Lennon is doing it is that he's on his honeymoon. I think we should see what the other three Beatles do before we get involved."

A senior from Princeton said, "We tried everything else. At least it'll be more fun than burning draft cards."

"I say let's do it," a Columbia militant shouted. "We could destroy the room service system in America overnight."

RED POWER INSTEAD OF BLACK POWER

Belsky, my Negro friend, was not impressed with the riot report that Governor Kerner and his commission issued.

"The trouble with the riot report," said Belsky, "is that there was no Communist threat implied in it."

"What on earth do you mean, Belsky?" I said.

"Congress isn't going to act on a report that doesn't have a Commie threat in it," Belsky said.

"But there were warnings in the report of riots and turmoil unless something is done about the ghettos."

"It's not the same thing," Belsky said. "You can talk about threats, frustration, inequities, poverty, joblessness, and anything you want to, but nobody is going to take notice unless you have a Communist menace thrown in somewhere."

"But that doesn't sound right," I said.

"Look, man, we're spending hundreds of millions of dollars each day out there in Vietnam to win the hearts and minds of people we don't even know or understand. Why? Because they are being threatened by Communism. Every time the President goes to Congress and says 'I've got to have a few billion dollars more, or else the Commies are going to take over that poor little country,' wham—he gets the money."

"Of course, and he should. You don't want to fight Communism on the shores of Hawaii, do you?" I said.

"No, sir. But what I'm trying to say is that you aren't going to get any action in this country until you can prove that the Commies are fighting to win the hearts and minds of the black people. You get that message over to Congress and they're not going to filibuster very long."

"Then you think if the Negro could prove that there is an international conspiracy to win over the Negroes to godless Communism, we might start a crash program to improve the conditions of the ghettos?" I said.

"I'm sure of it. America can live with poor people, it can live with jobless people, it can even live with angry people, but it can't live with Communist people. If the Negroes say to the Establishment, 'Hey, fellows, we got a Red threat in this here ghetto and we need some dollars to straighten it out,' there would be so many Brink trucks trying to deliver the money that there would be a traffic jam."

"It sounds good on paper, but would Congress go for it? After all, it's one thing to have a threat ten thousand miles away and help people out there improve their standard of living. But if you start doing the same thing in your own country, you're going to get an awful lot of people mad at you."

"I dig," Belsky said. "But the best record the United States has since World War II is in helping out any country threatened with Communism. When we make a commitment to a country to prevent it from going Communist, we honor it, no matter how much money it's going to cost. Now if the Negroes and the white do-gooders would stop talking about all the social ills in the ghettos and just harp on the theme that all the black people in this country want is to keep from going Communist, the white people are going to take a second look at this problem."

"It probably would make them sit up."

"You bet your life it would make them sit up. You go to Congress during an election year and talk about Red Power instead of Black Power and even George Wallace is going to be scared."

"Belsky, you may have hit on something. As a white American, I have nothing against black ghettos, but I sure wouldn't want to live in a country with Red ghettos."

"It's understandable," Belsky said. "Nobody wants to have a Commie living next door."

THE GOOD GUYS AND THE BAD

One of the major problems facing the United States in its racial troubles is trying to separate the good guys from the bad guys. White Americans tend to refer to all Negroes as "they," or worse. The Negroes use the term "whitey," or worse, to take in all the white people in the United States.

This becomes a problem, as I discovered not long ago when I had a conversation with a Negro acquaintance named Winslow.

"I see you people tried to burn down Washington last week," I said.

"Yes, but only after you people killed Martin Luther King."

"We didn't kill Martin Luther King. Some white nut did it."

"Well, I didn't burn down Washington," Winslow said. "I happened to be at home holding a bucket of water in case my house caught on fire."

"When I say 'you,'" I said, "I don't mean you, Winslow, I mean your people."

"What people are you talking about? I have to walk twenty blocks to buy a loaf of bread now. I can't even collect the insurance on my damaged car; my kids are afraid to go to school. Those cats weren't my people."

"I didn't exactly mean your people, Winslow," I tried to explain. "I meant people that look like you."

"Yeah, and what about your people? The reason we had all the trouble in the first place is that your people don't give a damn about what goes on in the ghettos until you have looting and riots."

"You can't make a general statement like that. A lot of white people care. You got to get it through your head, Winslow, that there are good white people and bad white people."

"Well, why don't you get it through your head that there are good black people and bad black people, and most of the black people don't dig rioting any more than the white people do?"

"If your people would stop supporting Stokely Carmichael and Rap Brown, it would be easier for us to be sympathetic to your problems."

"Then why don't the white people stop supporting Lester Maddox and George Wallace?"

"The white people don't support Maddox and Wallace. It's only a small minority that goes for them."

"How many black people do you think are doing cartwheels over Carmichael and Brown?" Winslow asked. "As a matter of fact, it's the white press that made them into our leaders. We never heard of them before."

"You're just trying to confuse me, Winslow," I protested. "I hear all you people have guns now."

"I don't have a gun and I never owned a gun. That's all I need with kids around the house. Whitey's got the guns."

"I don't have a gun either," I said angrily. "I got kids, too."

"I don't know what we're fighting about," Winslow said. "We both want to live in peace."

"Of course we do," I said, grabbing Winslow's hand. "You're a good Negro."

"And you're a good white man," Winslow said.

"You know what I'm going to do, Winslow, to show you how much I like you? I'm going to join the Urban League."

"And you know what I'm going to do in exchange?" Winslow said. "I'm going to join the Sons of the American Revolution. In that way we'll be soul brothers forever."

SOME SCARY STUDENT DEMANDS

As student demonstrations on campuses continue, the demands of the militants keep escalating. Some of the demands are reasonable, but others have built-in mousetraps. A few that I question have to do with student demands that universities take in people whether they're qualified or not, that all students who have flunked out be allowed to return to school, and that professors abolish the system of grading students for their courses.

I believe that in the liberal arts departments you might not have to be too concerned about high standards—you've seen one economics professor, you've seen them all—but it's in the sciences and professions that you can get a little tensed up.

If our future doctors, lawyers, engineers, and scientists no longer have to face stiff qualifying examinations or if the schools refuse to grade them on their abilities, some very weird situations might arise.

A patient goes into a doctor's office.

"What seems to be the trouble?" the doctor says.

"I have a pain in my side, Doctor."

"I don't know anything about pains in the side."

"I thought you were a medical doctor. At least that diploma says so."

"Are you some kind of racist?"

"No, I'm a patient."

"Well, it so happens I am a medical doctor. I just didn't do very well in anatomy. Never cared much for it. As a matter of fact, we locked up the dean of the medical school until he agreed to drop anatomy as a required course. We got him to do away with biology, also."

"But if you didn't like anatomy or biology, why did you become an M.D.?"

"A man has to be something."

Meanwhile, across town, a man was being tried for first-degree murder, and his lawyer and he were listening to the prosecutor.

"I want you, ladies and gentlemen, to send this man to the chair."

The defendant turns to his lawyer and asks, "Can he do that to me?"

The lawyer shrugs. "Beats hell out of me."

"But you're my lawyer. Don't you know what the law says?"

"I never told anyone this before, but I never really cared much for law. Matter of fact, all during school I had this girl and she had an apartment and—"

"Look, I don't care about your girl. My life is at stake. If I lose, will you at least make an appeal?"

"What's an appeal? You start studying about all this legal mumbo jumbo in college and you won't have any social life at all."

"But the law says—" the defendant cried.

"What does the law say? And don't go too fast because I want to write all this down. I never did take notes in school."

The third scene could take place twenty years from now at the new Major John V. Lindsay Bridge connecting Long Island with Connecticut.

The engineer is standing on the platform with the dignitaries.

"Well, Mr. Doubleday, you built a mighty fine bridge."

"That's my job."

"It seems to be sagging at one end. Is that the way it's supposed to be?"

"I'll build the bridges—you cut the ribbon."

"Look, there goes the first truck over the bridge—it's falling. *Doubleday, the entire bridge is falling!"*

"Sorry about that. I never could figure out how to use a slide rule."

STUDENT POWER

I hadn't realized the extent of student power in this country until I had dinner at a friend's house one evening not long ago. Among the guests seated at the table were a well-known TV newscaster, the head of a Congressional committee, a syndicated columnist, and the editor of a national magazine. An added starter was the nineteen-year-old son of one of the guests, who had just finished his freshman year at Amherst. We shall call him Stephen. Although it went against protocol, the hostess insisted that Stephen sit on her right.

As Stephen was cutting his meat, we all watched him nervously, hoping some pearls would drop out of his mouth. But when he didn't say anything, the Congressman jumped in.

"Tell me, Stephen," he said, "what do your friends think about the negative income tax?"

Stephen looked up in surprise. "I haven't heard them discuss it, though I imagine they're for it."

"Well put," the Congressman said.

"Let me ask you this, Stephen," the syndicated columnist said. "Does your generation believe the present revolutionary forces now at work throughout the world can produce a viable solution to the problems of pestilence, famine, and leisure?"

"I don't think you can generalize about student revolutions," Stephen replied.

The columnist wrote this down in a small notebook.

"Stephen," the TV commentator said. "If we grant you that *The Graduate* was a condemnation of our materialistic bourgeois society, would you grant us that there are some good things in *Gone with the Wind?*"

"I think there is some good in all movies," Stephen said. "As a matter of fact, many of my friends enjoyed *Gone with the Wind.*"

Everyone in the room seemed pleased.

The editor then asked Stephen, "How do we get out of Vietnam?"

Stephen said, "You just get out. It's that simple."

The Congressman shook his head in amazement. "That could be the solution. It just could."

We were eating our salad, and Stephen muttered something.

Everyone looked up. "What did he say? What did he say?"

"He said, 'Please pass the salt.'"

"Boy," said the columnist, "these kids really are bright these days."

"Our generation never asked anyone to pass the salt," the TV commentator said.

"We didn't have the guts," the Congressman said. "When the kids today want salt, they ask for it. That's student power."

Every one passed Stephen the salt.

Some started discussing the elections in France.

"Maybe Stephen doesn't want to talk about the elections in France," the magazine editor said.

"I don't really care one way or another," Stephen said.

"Well, how do you feel about the elections, Stephen?"

"I guess they went okay, considering."

"Tell us about pot," someone begged.

"I know kids who have smoked it," Stephen said.

"What did I tell you?" the columnist said. "He even knows about pot."

"I'd prefer to hear Stephen's views on the elections," the editor said.

"Why don't we wait until the men go into the library for coffee and cigars?"

"Not on your life," one of the women said. "We're just as interested to hear what Stephen has to say about politics as the men are. After all, you don't get a student to come to dinner every night."

THE UNDERSTANDING PROFESSOR

One of the things that impresses people about the student demonstrations is the strong stand that some members of the faculty take on the issues.

I was on the campus of Northamnesty University and

ran into a professor who was trying to stop his nose from bleeding. His clothes were torn up, and he was walking with a pronounced limp.

"What happened, Professor?" I asked, as I helped him search for his glasses.

"The militant students just took over my office and threw me down the stairs."

"Why, that's terrible!" I said.

"From *my* point of view it is, but I think we have to look at it from *their* point of view. Why did they throw me down the stairs? Where have we, as faculty, failed them?"

"Are you going to press charges?"

"On the contrary. If I pressed charges, I would only be playing into the hands of the repressive forces outside the university who would like nothing better than to see the students arrested for assault."

"But they did assault you?"

"Yes. I have to admit I was surprised about that. But there was one heartening note. As they threw me down the stairs, one of the students yelled, 'It isn't you, Professor. It's the system.' "

"That must have made you feel better."

"As I was tumbling down, the thought did occur to me that at least there was nothing personal in it."

"Say, Professor, isn't that the philosophy building going up in flames?"

"I believe it is. Now why did they have to go and set fire to the philosophy building?"

"I was going to ask you that."

"I'm not quite sure, because I haven't seen any of the students since they threw me down the stairs. My guess is that it probably has to do with something the administration and the students are at odds about."

"But that's a terrible thing to do."

"I don't think we should make judgments until all facts are in. I would say burning down a philosophy building could be interpreted as an unlawful act. At the same time, there are moments when an unlawful act can bring about just reforms."

"But the books, the records, the papers all are going up in smoke. Shouldn't we at least call the fire department?"

"I don't believe the fire department should be called until the faculty has met and voted on what course of action should be taken. There are times when a fire department can only inflame a situation. We should also hear from the students who started the fire and get their side of it. After all, they have as much stake in the university as anyone else, and if they don't want a philosophy building, we should at least listen to their arguments."

"I never thought of it that way," I admitted. "Professor, I know you can't see very well without your glasses, but I believe the militant students over at the quadrangle are building a scaffold. They wouldn't hang anyone, would they?"

"They haven't before," the professor said. "But it's quite possible that this is their way of seeking a confrontation with the Establishment."

As we were talking, a group of students rushed up and grabbed the professor. "We got one here," the ringleader shouted. "Get the rope."

"Don't worry, Professor," I shouted as I was pushed away by the mob. "I'll get the police."

"I wish you wouldn't," he said calmly as the students led him toward the scaffold. "If we don't let the students try new methods of activism, they'll never know for themselves which ones work and which ones are counterproductive."

HE GOT HIS NOTICE

"You'd better get over to the Diamonds' right away," my wife said when I came home one night.

"What's the trouble?"

"I don't know, but they sounded terribly upset."

I dashed over to the Diamond house and found Larry and Janet in the living room looking as if the world had fallen apart.

"What is it?" I asked.

"Billy got his draft notice," Janet said.

"He's been drafted?"

"It's worse," Larry said. "He's just been accepted for college."

"That couldn't be so bad."

"He's been accepted at the University of Wisconsin," Janet cried.

I didn't know what to say.

Larry shook his head. "You work all your life for your children, and then one day, out of the blue, they grab them and that's it."

"But even if they accepted him, he doesn't have to go," I said.

"You don't understand," Janet said. "He *wants* to go. He said he can't sit at home doing nothing when so many college kids are sacrificing so much on the campuses."

Larry said, "He wants to be where the action is."

"Billy always had a sense of duty," I said.

"I tried to talk him into going into the Army instead," Larry told me. "But he said, 'Dad, I would be shirking my responsibilities. That's the coward's way out. I have to go where my friends are fighting.'"

Janet sobbed, "I told him to go into the Army for four years, and then perhaps the fighting on the campuses would be over. But he said, 'Mother, I could never face my children if they asked me someday what I did during the war on campus and I had to tell them I was in the Army while it was going on.'"

"You have to be proud of him," I said.

"What do you mean, proud?" Larry said. "It's fool-hardy. He doesn't know what he's getting into. All he sees is the glamor of it. The blue jeans and the dirty sweater and the beard. But I told him there's more to going to college than that. College is a dirty, miserable business, and it isn't just bands playing and flags waving and girls kissing you in the dormitories."

Janet nodded her head sadly. "I guess he saw too many TV programs about college riots and it went to his head."

Larry said, "Even as a little boy he always had his heart set on college. He used to stage sit-ins in the kitchen, and he picketed our bedroom at night, and once he locked his grandfather in the bathroom because his grandfather wouldn't grant him amnesty for using a naughty word.

"I thought it was a stage all kids go through, so I didn't take it seriously. If I had known he was truly thinking of going to college, I certainly wouldn't have encouraged it."

I tried to cheer my friends up. "Maybe he'll be all right.

Don't forget, not everybody who goes to college gets
arrested. If he comes out of it without a criminal record,
it could be a very broadening experience. Why, some kids
even get an education from college."

Janet was really crying. "You're just saying that to buck
us up. You really don't believe it, do you?"

I looked at the distraught couple. "I have friends at the
University of Wisconsin," I told them. "Perhaps I could
use my influence to get Billy into night school. Then, at
least, he'll be safe."

GOODCHEER'S FINEST HOUR

It was bound to happen. The students of Goodcheer
University, after having attained all their goals, had nothing more to demonstrate about. They called a mass meeting on the quadrangle in front of the administration building.

"Students," yelled Hardin Helrazor, "we have run out
of demands. The administration has given in to our every
wish, and if we don't come up with something soon, we
may have to go back to classes."

Loud booing.

"Why can't we demand that boys and girls live in the
same rooms?" a student shouted.

"They can, stupid," another student shouted. "We got
that privilege when we locked up the football coach for
three days in the shower room."

"Why don't we demand that no teacher can be hired
without first going through a year of hazing at one of the
fraternities?" another student said.

"Idiot, that was put through after we burned down the
science building," Helrazor said.

"Oh, I thought we burned down the science building
because they wouldn't give us a coffee break during tests."

"No, we got the coffee break after we kidnapped the
dean of men."

"Come on, students, don't just stand there with your
tongues sticking out," Helrazor said. "There must be
something we want that they haven't given us."

"What about parking space?" a co-ed cried. "We don't
have enough parking space."

"We got them to tear down the medical school to give us more parking space," Helrazor said. "It would be hard to go back to them again with that one."

"Free love in the library," someone shouted.

"We're allowed to have free love in the library now."

"Yeah, but you have to show your student union card. If it's free, it should be free for nonstudents, as well as students."

"Let's kidnap the dean of the law school, and let *them* come up with some ideas," a bearded youth yelled.

"Yeah," his companion shouted. "Why should we have to think up our demands all the time? The school has a responsibility to make some up for us."

Loud cheering.

Helrazor said, "That's playing the administration's game. They'd love to think up student demands they could give in to. But what kind of demonstration is that? I say this time we have to go for broke. They've got to believe we mean business. Otherwise, they'll have us back in those classes studying all that garbage. Is that what we came to college for?"

Chorus: "No!"

"I've got it. I've got it. Let's hold a demonstration protesting the fact that administration has given in to all our demands," a student said.

"They're patronizing us."

"They've taken our pride away from us."

Muttering from the crowd.

"We're sick and tired of living in a permissive society."

Helrazor tried to restore order. "It may work. We'll lock the dean of women in the drama department and won't let her out unless the university takes disciplinary action against us. We want our manhood back."

"If they give us an amnesty, we'll tear the faculty club apart."

After the dean of women was held for four days, the administration of Goodcheer University finally gave in and agreed to punish all the troublemakers in the school.

It was the demonstrators' finest hour. Goodcheer has been served notice that if, in the future, they refuse to discipline any student for an infraction, the student union will be burned to the ground.

THE GOOD STUDENTS AND THE BAD

It is generally agreed that student unrest is worldwide. It doesn't matter if the students live in a permissive society or a totalitarian one—they're still raising Cain. And for that reason, those of us watching from the sidelines are divided on whether the unrest is a good thing or a bad thing.

One day, at the University Club, I was having a brandy and cigar with some very nice chaps when the question of student demonstrations came up.

"I see where they're still having problems at Columbia," Liverwhistle said.

"It's appalling, absolutely appalling," Cartwright sputtered.

"The students all should be booted out on their ears. You can't have a university if you're going to have children running around locking up the faculty."

Conrad said, "Did you read what's going on in Paris? The French students have tied up the city."

"Ah, yes," said Cartwright. "One can't help admiring the French students' gumption. They've certainly put De Gaulle in his place."

"You have to respect their attitude," Liverwhistle said. "At least the students can see through De Gaulle, if the rest of the French people can't."

"I don't think things have cooled off at Stanford," Studsdale commented. They're still holding the administration building."

"If you ask me," said Cartwright, "it's a Communist plot. These things don't just happen. There's nothing the Commies wouldn't do to shut down the schools in this country. The only answer is force. It will make those radicals sing another tune."

"Did you read where the students in Czechoslovakia not only demonstrated, but caused the downfall of the Soviet-backed regime?"

"God bless them," said Conrad. "If we're ever going to see the end of tyranny behind the Iron Curtain, it's going to be the students who accomplish it."

"I understand the same thing could happen in Poland," Liverwhistle said, "and perhaps even East Germany.

They're a new breed, those students, and a credit to the human race."

"You know, of course," said Studsdale, "that the administration completely collapsed at Northwestern and gave in to every demand of the students there."

Cartwright said, "My blood boiled when I read the story. Those damn kids don't know up from down, and they're telling us how to run the country. I say we have to act now and act firmly. We ought to cut off all funds to any student who demonstrates or strikes against a university administration."

"The students in Franco's Spain have been agitating for a year now. No one knows how many are in jail," Conrad said.

"The poor kids," Liverwhistle said. "They're only trying to make a better world, and they're thrown in jail for it. I think we should get up a petition and send it to the Spanish ambassador."

"I see they're having another sit-in at Berkeley," Liverwright commented.

"They're always having a sit-in at Berkeley," Studsdale said.

"I'll tell you what's wrong with the kids today. They've got too much money. They don't even appreciate what we've gone through to give them an education. All they talk about is freedom. What kind of freedom do they want?"

"It's the faculty," said Conrad. "They're the ones who egg the students on. Instead of jailing students, they ought to lock up the faculty. Then we'd stop all this anarchy on campuses."

Cartwright, who was flipping through a newspaper, said, "It says here that the students in Communist China are thinking about having another Red Guard revolution."

"Great," said Liverwhistle. "Old Mao won't be able to take another one of those."

Liverwright agreed. "I must say one thing for the students abroad. They sure have a lot of class."

UP AGAINST THE WALL

Those of us who try to keep abreast of student affairs have noticed that student riots are taking on a pattern. The script reads something like this:

Dean of students arrives on campus. Students start throwing rocks, dirt, and tomatoes at him and try to hit him over the head as they scream, "Amnesty! Amnesty!"

Dean of students, as he tries to protect himself, yells back, "What do you want amnesty from?"

Students: "From attacking you. We demand that you sign a paper that we won't be punished for throwing things at you and trying to hit you over the head."

Dean: "But why should I do that? Wouldn't it be better if you didn't attack me?"

Students: "Spoken like a bourgeois racist. You don't even care to listen to what we have to say."

Dean: "I'd be happy to hear what you've got to say, if you'd just stop throwing things at me. I can't listen when I'm constantly ducking."

Students: "Obscenity—what do you have to say to that?"

Dean: "I didn't understand the question."

Students: "You don't want to understand the question. Obscenity, obscenity, obscenity."

Dean: "Very interesting."

Students: "What about the draft?"

Dean: "I don't know anything about the draft. My specialty is anthropology."

Students: "Black is beautiful."

Dean: "That's very good. Why are you throwing that chair at me?"

Students: "The system stinks and we have nothing to say about the crummy, capitalistic, profit-making Establishment."

Dean: "I assure you that whether you throw that chair at me or not, it is not going to help your cause. It could even hurt it."

Students: "We don't have a cause. We have certain demands and if they're not met in two hours, we're going to burn down the library."

Dean: "What good will that do?"

Students: "It will bring about the needed reforms in education."

Dean: "Without books?"

Students: "You're trying to hold a dialogue with us."

Dean: "Heaven forbid."

Students: "If you don't agree to sign a paper giving us amnesty, we'll close down the school."

Dean: "I don't have the authority to give you amnesty. But I won't press any charges against you, if you'll stop hitting me with those table legs."

Students: "You're patronizing us. Aren't we even grown up enough to have charges pressed against us?"

Dean: "All right. I'll press charges against you then, if that's what you want."

Students: "We knew you would, you South Vietnamese puppet."

Dean: "Now you've gone too far. You're all suspended from this school."

Students: "What about due process? Don't we even get a trial?"

Dean: "You will, after you're all expelled."

Students: "Up against the wall! Up against the wall!"

Dean: "You said it; I didn't."

Students: "Don't we have any constitutional rights at all?"

WHAT IS WRONG WITH PARENTS?

A panel of distinguished students met at Wavering University recently to discuss the pressing topic of the day: What is wrong with parents?

Cal Holden said the restlessness and unhappiness attributed to most parents these days could be blamed on the fact that students have been too permissive with their parents.

"We haven't stood up to them," he said. "We let them buy us cars and clothes and pay our tuition and give us vacations, and the more we let them do for us, the more surly and unmanageable they become."

Mary Beth Lou agreed. "When you spare the rod, you spoil the mother. I find parents are so much happier when you tell them what *you* want to do, instead of asking them what they want to do. Parents are like children. They need discipline. I have a great relationship with my parents only because when my father and mother get out of line, I let them know it."

Dick Duncan said, "It seems to me that parents have too much money to spend. Everything's too easy for them. They have no real values. I think you would have to blame the economy for this. Advertisers are constantly appealing to parents. Because of their purchasing power, parents are made to think they're important, and they get an inflated opinion of themselves. Parents believe, since they are so sought after by the advertiser, that they know everything."

Sherry Cerf was one of the few to dissent with the panel.

"I think we're doing too much generalizing about parents. The minority of activist parents gives the majority of parents a bad name. I think you'll find the average parent reasonable and interested in most things. Oh, they have kooky ideas about pot and sex, but when it gets to serious matters, I find them level-headed."

Larry Massee said, "It seems to me the inability to get through to parents is a communications gap, and students are to blame. We never ask where parents are going or what time they're coming back. When they try to tell their problems, we ignore them and pretend they're inconsequential. But their problems, no matter how minor they seem to us, are important to them. Most students spend so much time demonstrating and defying the college administrations that they don't have any time to devote to their own mothers and fathers."

"Larry's right," Esther Bird declared. "And I have a good illustration to prove it. The other night my father told me his business was bankrupt and he would have to go on relief. Now that didn't seem important to me, but for some reason it seemed important to him. So I listened to his problem, and he felt so much better afterward because I showed an interest. It's little things like this that build bridges between students and their bewildered parents."

"Red" Schaefer was not convinced. "The sociologists and psychologists are making too much of parents being confused and unhappy. All parents are unhappy, or they wouldn't be parents. Instead of catering to them every time they complain about something, we should say to them, 'Until we're out of the house and able to make our own living, you have to go along with what we say and do or we'll just move out!' It's a futile exercise to try to appease parents who don't know what they want in the first place."

Herb Sargent added: "I think we have to face up to the fact, whether we like it or not, that parents will be the biggest problem of the next generation. I suggest that we set up a study group to find out, first, how deep parent discontent is; second, what remedies can be taken to keep this discontent from getting out of hand; and third, ways of channeling adult activism into socially acceptable patterns."

The proposal was adopted unanimously, and the Ford Foundation agreed to underwrite it.

OH, TO BE A SWINGER

It's very hard for many college students to live up to the roles they have been given by the mass media. What newspapers, magazines, and television networks expect from students is more than most of them can deliver. I discovered this when I was speaking at a Midwestern campus not long ago.

A student, whom I shall call Ronald Hoffman, seemed very troubled and I asked him what the problem was.

"My parents are coming up next week, and I don't know what to do."

"Why?"

"Well, you see, I told them I was living off campus with this co-ed in an apartment. But the truth is that I'm living in the dormitory."

"That shouldn't really disturb them."

"Oh, but it will. They're very proud of me, and they think I should have a mind of my own. When my dad heard I was living off campus with a co-ed, he doubled my allowance because, as he put it, 'Anyone who is willing to spit in the eye of conformity deserves his father's support.' I don't know what he's going to say when he finds out I used the money to buy books."

"It'll hurt him," I agreed. "What will your mother say?"

"I don't know. She's been crying a lot since I wrote her

about living with this co-ed, and Dad's been arguing with her that her trouble is she doesn't understand youth. Mom's likely to get pretty sore when she discovers she's been crying for nothing."

"Not to mention how silly your father will look for making her cry."

Ronald shook his head sadly. "The trouble with parents these days is they believe everything they read. *Life* magazine, in a 'Sex on the Campus' article, made it sound so easy to find a co-ed to live with. Well, let me tell you, for every girl who's playing house with a male college student, there are a million co-eds who won't even do the dishes."

"Then all this talk of students living out of wedlock is exaggerated?"

"Exaggerated? When I got here, I asked ten girls if they wanted to live with me. The first one said she didn't come to college to iron shirts for the wrong guy, four told me frankly that it would hurt their chances of finding a husband, four told me to drop dead, and one reported me to the campus police. I was lucky to get a room in the dormitory."

"I guess it's no fun for a young man to pretend he's a swinger."

"You can say that again. Every time I go home, everybody wants to know about the pot parties and orgies I go to at school. The only thing that's saved me is that I've seen *La Dolce Vita* twice."

"You have to depend on your imagination?"

"What college boy doesn't?" Ronald said. "There are more conscientious objectors amongst co-eds in the sexual revolution than any modern sociologist would dare admit."

"It's enough to destroy your faith in Hugh Hefner," I said.

"Look, I'm not complaining," Ronald said. "I'm just trying to figure out how to explain it to my father. He's living his fantasies through me, and I hate to let him down."

"Why don't you tell him the reason you can't introduce the co-ed you're living with is that she's going to have a baby?"

"Hey," Ronald said, "that's a great idea. It might cause Mom to cry again, but it will make Dad awfully proud."

HUNGER STRIKE

A parent never knows what kind of call he's going to get these days from his offspring in college. One evening a friend of mine received a call from his daughter who attends a small Midwest school.

"Hello, Daddy," she said. "Guess what? I'm on a hunger strike."

My friend gulped. "That's wonderful, Martha. How long have you been on it?"

"Two days. I'm starving."

"Where are you calling from?" my friend asked.

"The dorm. Almost all the girls here are on the strike, too."

"Isn't that nice?" My friend gulped again. "Tell me, what are you striking about?"

"Just a minute," his daughter said—and then he heard her say to someone next to her, "What are we striking about?"

A moment later she replied, "We're on a hunger strike because they're recruiting on campus."

"Who's recruiting on campus?"

"What do you mean who's recruiting on campus?"

"Are you striking against companies who are recruiting on campus or military recruiting?"

"Hold it," she said. In the background he could hear her say, "Who are we striking against? Commercial recruiters or military recruiters?"

She came back on the line. "It's commercial, Daddy. They want people to join the Dow Chemical Company."

"How long do you expect to be on your hunger strike?" my friend asked.

"How long are we going to be on the hunger strike?" he heard his daughter ask somone.

There was a pause, and she came back on the line. "Nobody knows. This is the first time anyone's done it."

"Can't you give me some idea?" my friend said.

He could hear her talking with people in the background. "Susie said that Gandhi went for sixty days without eating or drinking anything but orange juice."

"But he was in training," my friend said. "He deescalated his food intake for months before he struck."

He heard his daughter say to her friends, "He says Gandhi trained for his hunger strike."

More background talking. Then his daughter came on: "That's what we were calling you about. How long do you think we should stay on it?"

"I'm flattered that you'd ask me," my friend said, "but frankly, I've never been involved in a hunger strike myself. I thought you kids usually took over the administration building."

"It doesn't have the impact of a hunger strike. You should see the president of the school. He's practically in tears. Our cheeks are all sallow, and we groan a lot. The president knows how to deal with student sit-ins, but he has no idea what to do with kids who are starving themselves to death."

"Well, I'm very proud of you," my friend said. "You're certainly sticking up for your principles. I'd say I'd give it another day, and then you'll have made your point."

He heard his daughter tell her friends, "He says to give it another day and then we'll have made our point." Pause—then she came on the line. "Do you mean another day, like tomorrow, or twenty-four hours from like now, when I'm talking to you?"

My friend pretended to weigh the choice. "I would say twenty-four hours from now."

His daughter repeated the decision, and my friend heard a cheer go up from the dorm. "Thanks, Dad. We'll never forget what you've done for us."

THE INFORMER

Even in the politics of confrontation, where everyone is up against the wall, there comes a moment of truth. It could come in a darkened, off-campus apartment where everyone is sitting around smoking pot and talking about Chicago. Or it could come on the steps of Columbia University at high noon during homecoming week. For my friend Tom Busted, the moment of truth came one day as he was addressing a group of student revolutionaries in a basement on a plan to blow out all telephones in the United States.

"Now this is my plan," Busted said. "Every student in America—and there are eleven million of us—will make a telephone call at exactly the same time. It will blow out every fuse in the United States, and without telephones, the whole blank-blank bourgeois, blank system in the country will collapse."

"What a blanking idea," one of the revolutionaries cried. "We've been blanking around the campuses when we should have been wrecking the telephone company."

"Beautiful," another revolutionary yelled. "And it's legal. No one can bust us for making a telephone call."

"But," said another revolutionary, "if it's legal, do we want to do it? I thought the revolution had to come about by breaking all the blanking laws."

"Sometimes," said Tom, "even in a revolution, you have to do something legal to bring down the Establishment."

"Let's hear it for Tom," a revolutionary said.

The group cheered wildly.

"Thanks a lot, brothers," Tom said. "But let's get on with the meeting. It's my birthday, and my girl is baking me a cake."

"Hey, why didn't you tell us? Happy birthday, Tom."

"Yeah, happy birthday, Tom. Let's hear it for Tom's birthday."

They sang it, ending with "happy birthday, blanking Tom, happy birthday to you."

"How old are you, Tommy baby?"

"I'm . . . I'm . . . I'm thirty."

There was a dead silence in the basement.

"Thirty?" one of the revolutionaries said menacingly. "You dirty, rotten informer."

"What's the matter with you guys?" Busted yelled. "What did I say?"

"Here you were pretending you were one of us. We trusted you, we were willing to lay down our lives for you. And all the time you were giving us this jazz, you knew you were thirty years old."

"You're one of them!" a revolutionary shouted.

"I'm not one of them. I'm one of you," Tom protested. "It's not my fault I'm thirty years old."

"You sold out."

"I didn't sell out. I'm the same guy I was when I was twenty-nine. George, Max, Eddie, Joe, Jerry, you've known me for eight years. Am I different? I ask you."

"You're nothing but an old blankety pig."

"I say we split his head open."

"Put sugar in his gas tank."

"Slash his tires."

Tom was almost in tears. "Please, let me prove I haven't sold out. I'll burn my draft card again; I'll put a Vietcong flag on the top of the Pentagon; I'll even hijack the football team's airplane. Let me show you I haven't changed."

Finally, one of the revolutionaries said, "Don't trust anyone over thirty. You told us that yourself."

"But that was five years ago," Tom protested, "when I was twenty-five. I think we ought to move it up to, let's say, thirty-five. Don't trust anyone over thirty-five. How about that?"

"Turn in your Che Guevara button, Tom."

"No, not my Che Guevara button," Tom cried.

"Now get out of here, and if we ever see you at a student demonstration again, we'll shove a Mao Tse-tung placard right down your throat."

Tom walked out of the basement a pitiful, shaken old man, with nothing to look forward to but Medicare.

A HECKLERS' CONVENTION

Heckling of speakers has become such a big thing on college campuses these days that it has been decided to hold an Intercollegiate Hecklers' Conference in the near future.

The man behind it is Hiram Bullhorn, who came to Washington to arrange for speakers who could be heckled at the conference.

"We were hoping to get President Nixon," Hiram said, "but we may have to settle for Spiro Agnew and General Hershey."

"What do you intend to do at the conference?"

"We want to exchange ideas on heckling, discuss new methods of jeering and hooting, and see if we can find ways of shedding more heat and less light on the basic issues of the day."

"It should be very constructive," I said.

"I've had a very good response. Almost every university in the country wants to send a delegation. That is, if they don't have any speakers to heckle on their campuses the week of the convention."

"How do you intend to conduct the conference?"

"We'll break it down into seminars. One group will discuss 'heckling from the balcony,' another 'heckling from the floor,' and a third, for graduate students, will devote itself to 'what to do if you can grab the mike.'

"We will also hold a session on 'new jeers' and classes in 'dirty sign painting.' And we shall probably devote an entire afternoon to 'what to do about antiheckling.' "

"What do you mean by 'antiheckling'?"

"Well, for some time hecklers were permitted to heckle without being interrupted. But now the speakers have been heckling the hecklers. Muskie embarrassed students by giving them time to state their cases. Humphrey hooted at kids in the balcony. Wallace told the TV men to turn their cameras on the hecklers to embarrass them, and even Nixon has used hecklers to get sympathy for himself.

"This antiheckling behavior of the speakers has caused a great deal of resentment among activist students and is a violation of the First Amendment, which guarantees to all citizens the right to hoot and jeer without fear of having to listen to what someone has to say."

"But what can you do about it?"

"We will probably call for legislation to make antiheckling illegal, and we shall train student leaders in anti-antiheckling techniques. This will include cutting off microphones, the use of larger hand megaphones, and the escalation of catcalling. If we can't stop someone from speaking without their answering back, then free speech in this country has come to a sorry pass."

"I couldn't agree with you more. Where will you hold your first hecklers' convention?"

"Everyone wants it. Berkeley has asked for it; Columbia has lobbied for it; Madison, Wisconsin, says they'll host it; but we think the only place to have a convention in this country is Chicago. For one thing, they have the best facilities for hecklers, and for another, after all the unfortunate publicity Mayor Daley got after the Democratic Convention, he deserves the business."

8

Have Gun,
Will Travel

CRIME AND NATIONAL POLICY

The crime problem in Washington, D.C., as everyone knows, is serious. And everyone is worried about it because it could have an effect on the national policies of the country. It's very difficult for people to make decisions on the affairs of state when they are living in an atmosphere of apprehension and anxiety.

Let me explain what I mean.

Not long ago I was getting a briefing on America's defense posture from my good friend General A. B. Em at the Pentagon.

"The United States has never been stronger, in spite of everything you read," General Em told me. "We've got hardware in every part of the globe, and while we're not looking for trouble, I assure you that there isn't a nation in the world, including you know who, who would mess with us. But of course, our real business is peace."

"It's good to talk to someone who is neither a dove nor a hawk," I said.

"Without giving away any secret information, our missile sites right here in the continental United States could knock out anything the other side could send over."

An aide walked in. "I'm sorry to bother you, sir, but your car has been stolen."

"My car!"

"Yes, sir. Right off the Pentagon parking lot."

"Of all the nerve," the general shouted. He put on his coat and said to me, "I'm sorry I have to break this up." And then, to his aide, "Let's go ahead with the bombing raid on the DMZ. And double the bomb loads."

I wandered over to State to see if I could talk a friend on the Middle East desk into having lunch. He was wrestling with the tricky situation out there. "It's our policy to find a peaceful solution to this problem, making sure that neither the Arabs nor the Israelis feel they've won anything. But at the same time we must calm the fears of both parties and urge them to reconcile their differences."

Just then his secretary came in. "It's your wife on the phone." He picked it up. "Hello ... What do you mean someone broke into the house? They took everything? ... I know you wanted me to put bars on the windows ... Will you calm down? ... Yes, I'm coming home right away." He slammed down the phone.

"What about the position paper you were going to do on the crisis?" his secretary asked.

My friend was heading for the door. "The hell with the position paper. The Arabs and Israelis can kill themselves for all I care." And he walked out, slamming the door.

I had nothing better to do, so I decided to look up a pal at the Department of Housing and Urban Development. He was just going over plans for a large housing project for one of the major cities. "What we have to do is give people decent housing," he said.

"Once we can improve the environment, we will be able to deal with the problems of the underprivileged and disenfranchised. Now this model program, if it works, could be repeated in every part of the country and—"

"Mr. Bostitch." A uniformed guard rushed in. "They just robbed the employees' credit union downstairs and took twenty thousand dollars."

"That does it!" said Bostitch as he tore up the plans into little pieces. "No more Mr. Nice Guy."

I was about to go back to my office when I ran into a judge. "We must get to the root of crime and eradicate the causes of it," he said as he walked back to his court. "Punishing people is not a solution for the long haul." In his chambers he said to his clerk, "Where's my robe?"

"Someone stole it during lunch."

Red-faced, the judge took his seat on the bench in his regular suit, and before the defense attorney could even make his plea in the first case, the judge slammed down his gavel and said, "Twenty years."

GETTING AWAY FROM IT ALL

Whenever I get discouraged about the world situation, I go to Martha's Vineyard, that lovely isle of green off the good Cape of Cod. Here people have learned to live in harmony and peace, and everybody gets along with everybody else, with only a few exceptions.

"Can't stand the people on the mainland," a fellow in the drugstore said to me as we were drinking a malted milk together.

"Don't blame you," I said.

"You living up-island or down-island?"

"Down-island," I confessed.

"Wrong place to live. Up-island people are much nicer than down-island people. Friendlier—not so stuck up."

"But the island's only seventeen miles long."

"Exactly;" he said. "There's a lot of difference in people living seventeen miles apart."

"I'll move," I said.

"Don't make much difference," he said. "Even if you moved up-island, the people who live there all year round wouldn't have any use for you. They don't like people who come here in the summer and spoil everything."

"But we're just trying to get some rest."

"That's the point. You're resting, and they have to work. You rent or own?" he asked.

"I rent."

"I thought so," he said. "You look like someone who rents."

"Does it show?"

"Certainly. People who own can tell people who rent a mile away. We don't have much use for people who rent."

"I'm thinking of buying."

"Where?"

"In Vineyard Haven."

"Low class of people buy in Vineyard Haven. Hardly anybody worth knowing lives there."

"There are a lot of writers who live in Vineyard Haven."

"We don't think much of writers around here. They're always taking ads out in the newspapers and writing letters to the editor trying to change things. You live among writers and no one in Edgartown will talk to you."

"Then people in Edgartown don't like people in Vineyard Haven?"

"Why should they? Edgartown has the best yacht club. You sail or motor?"

"Does it make any difference?"

"You must be joking. People who use sail hate people who use motor. We're trying to banish motorboats from the island."

"I like to sail," I pleaded.

"Ketch or catamaran?"

"Do I have to make a choice?"

"Yup. Ketch people have no truck with catamaran people."

I took another slug of malted milk. "I guess there is one thing everyone agrees on here," I said. "And that's the fishing."

"Are you kidding? The lobster people hate the sword fishermen and the mackerel people hate the lobstermen, and they all hate the clammers."

"You would think on a little island like this everyone would work together and love each other," I said.

The man looked at his glass. "They make much better malted milks in Chilmark."

"If you don't like it here, why don't you go back where you come from?" I said angrily.

"I used to live in Menemsha, thirteen miles down the road, but I had to move here because of my sinuses.

"People in Menemsha don't like people with sinus trouble. It gives the town a bad name."

GUN LOVERS ON THE DEFENSIVE

Wallaby Cartridge, the president of the National Gun Lovers of America and Bugle Corps, was enraged when I saw him in a restaurant one day spoon-feeding an Old-Fashioned into the mouth of a U.S. Senator.

"Americans are behaving like children," Wallaby said, "parroting nonsense, and trying to bring pressure on Congress to pass antigun legislation."

"But that's lobbying," I said in a shocked voice.

"You're damn right it's lobbying, and the National Gun Lovers of America through its lobby is officially protesting. There's a conspiracy going on to take guns away from the American people, and we won't stand for it—not after all the money and time we've spent preventing it. Senator, can I order you some caviar?"

The Senator nodded his head.

"What I don't understand, Wallaby, is why the American

people just won't take your word that guns don't kill people, people kill people."

"Because the American people are being brainwashed. They think they can prevent crime and keep guns out of the hands of criminals and adolescents and disturbed people by making Americans register their guns. But at the same time they don't realize how much inconvenience they would be causing the sincere hunter and marksman."

"Nobody wants to inconvenience people who hunt," I agreed.

"How about a nice steak, Senator?" Wallaby said.

He then continued. "Do you know one of the things they want to do? They want to pass a law forbidding the sale of long guns and shotguns through the mail. Do you realize what this would do to hunters? They'd have to go down to a store and buy the gun over the counter and give their names to the sales clerk."

"But that's outrageous. Hunters shouldn't be forced to go to a store to buy their guns. They've got too much to do, getting up at three in the morning and sitting in a duck blind for four hours in the mud, to find time to go to a store."

"I'm glad you understand it," Wallaby said. "But there's more to it than that. They want to take our guns away from us."

"Who does?"

"*They* do," Wallaby said, ominously.

"Then it's a conspiracy," I cried.

"Of course it's a conspiracy," Wallaby said. "Who do you think is behind all those letters being sent to Congressmen and Senators this week?"

"The American people?"

"You fool. The conspiracy's behind it. They know if they can get a list of the people in the United States who own guns, *they'll* be able to take over."

"And the only thing standing between *they* and us is *you*."

I thought Wallaby was going to burst into tears.

"Everything was going so well. We had Congress in our pocket. Our mail campaign for guns outnumbered the antigun mail by six to none. We had the thing in the bag. But now the mail is running against us, and everyone's blaming me. I've been a good lobbyist, a loyal lobbyist, a free-spending lobbyist. If they pass a strong antigun law, who would have me?"

My heart was breaking. "Maybe people will stop writing letters against guns," I said hopefully.

"It's too late." Wallaby shook his head.

"Then why are you entertaining this Senator?" I asked.

"I can't help it. It's the only thing I know how to do."

Wallaby shoved a cigar in the Senator's mouth and started to pour some brandy down his throat.

HAVE GUN, WILL TRAVEL

You would think after all the United States has done for Europe, the least the Europeans could do is make it easy for an American to buy a gun. But such is not the case. In spite of their great claims to being civilized, the Europeans are still living in the Dark Ages when it comes to making firearms available to the public.

I discovered this accidentally when I was overcharged by a waiter in a Left Bank café. He claimed it was an accident, but I knew he did it on purpose.

I told my wife I was getting sick and tired of being pushed around, and the only thing to do was buy a gun and carry it with me at all times. Then if someone tried to overcharge me, I'd let him have it.

"Isn't that a bit strong?" my wife asked.

"It's the American way," I said. "Can you think of a better reason for using a gun than when you get the business from a surly café waiter?"

The next day I went to a gun store near the Paris Opéra and told them I wanted a revolver.

"What do you want it for?" the dealer asked.

"I am an American citizen," I said, "and according to our Constitution, I am allowed to bear arms, any place, any time. Now be a good man and give me a gun."

"We cannot sell a gun just like that, monsieur," the dealer said. "We have regulations in France concerning guns."

"Regulations?" I said incredulously. "What on earth for?"

"The French government does not want everyone in the country to have a gun. There is too much chance of accidents."

"That doesn't bother us in the United States," I said with a certain amount of pride. "Do you know last year we had more than five thousand people killed by firearms alone?"

"Asla," said the dealer, sadly. "We only had twelve. The rules here are too strict."

"Don't you have a National Rifle Association?"

"We have something like it, but Parliament tells them what they can or cannot do."

"In my country," I boasted, "the National Rifle Association tells Congress what it can or cannot do."

"Quelle chance," the dealer said. "Please sir, what can I do for you?"

"I want a gun to shoot surly café waiters."

"Très bien, fill out these papers. Then go to your local police station with all your identification and explain to them why you want a gun."

"Good, and then I can have it?"

"No, not yet. They will investigate you for three months. After that, they will send their recommendation to the main police station, which will investigate why the local police station gave permission to let you have the gun. This will take three more months. If they agree, you can come back and buy the gun."

"Six months to buy one lousy gun?"

"That's for the gun. Buying ammunition requires another investigation."

"Do you know if we had red tape like that in America, almost nobody would be able to own a revolver?"

"That's why we don't sell too many ourselves," the dealer said. "Do you want to start filling out the papers?"

"No, I don't, and if the French had any sense they'd permit Americans to buy handguns just by showing their passport. How else can we protect ourselves from waiters while we're traveling abroad?"

THE COMMITTEE ON VIOLENCE

"The Subcommittee on Violence will come to order. Will someone please turn off that television set?"

"Sorry, I was fascinated by a commercial of two people kidnapping a car dealer and stealing the car. It's rather an extraordinary way to sell cars."

"Well, we don't have time to discuss that now. We have to get down to the business of violence. Senator, do you mind putting down that magazine? We're ready to begin the meeting. Senator—"

"Huh? Oh—excuse me. Look at this. Here is a carbine for sale by mail for only twenty-six dollars. How the blazes do they do it?"

"Probably some foreign make. My constituents are furious at the flood of foreign guns coming into this country."

"I don't blame them. If you're an American gun lover, the least you can do is buy American."

"Gentlemen, can we call this meeting to order? We're trying to get to the cause of violence and—"

"Listen, before we start, I saw a movie the other night and found it damned interesting. It was a cowboy picture, and it may have had a little too much blood for everybody's taste, but I never saw anything so realistic."

"Talk about realism. Did you see that shot of the soldier on the news last night on TV just as he got hit and—"

"This meeting must come to order immediately. We are here today to discuss the causes of violence in the United States."

"May I ask a question? Will we be done by four? If I don't get home early, my wife will kill me."

"Knowing your wife, she would, too."

"May I repeat, gentlemen, we're here to discuss violence. Let's not get off the track."

"Well, can we get on with it? I've got an election coming up, and if I don't murder my opponent in the primary, I'm a dead duck."

"Let's not talk politics now. We have to think of witnesses we want to call."

"I hope we come up with something concrete because I have to give a graduation speech and I've been beating my brains out trying to think of something to say."

"If you don't beat your brains out, the students will do it for you."

"Very funny."

"We're getting off the subject again, gentlemen."

"I'd like to say one thing before we get started. We can't keep the secretaries on the committee late unless we can escort them home by the police."

"I'm not sure the police will agree to that."

"But how are we going to get the report out on time?"

"We could work Saturdays."

"That's no good. I'm going hunting on Saturday."

"We'll face that problem when we come to it."

"I believe that the first thing we should do is write a preface to the report deploring violence."

"That's a stupid idea."

"Don't call me stupid unless you want to step outside."

"Order, order! Can't we keep our feelings under control?"

"If I'm going to work on this committee, I demand respect."

"Drop dead."

"It looks as if we're not going to get anywhere today. Let's adjourn until tomorrow."

"Good idea. It will give us a chance to read up on why people are always resorting to violence."

VISIT THE U.S.A.

Dear Visitor from Abroad:

This is your invitation to visit the U.S.A., otherwise known as the Land of Bonnie and Clyde.

To make it easier for you, we will answer some of the questions that foreign tourists keep asking us.

"Is it dangerous to visit the United States?"

Of course not. Americans are a gentle people who abhor violence. What little there is can be seen on television or in the movies—every night. We have cowboy films, cops and robbers pictures, and children's cartoons. If that isn't your cup of tea, you can tune in on one of our news shows. We show not only people being killed, but villages being burned, GI's being wounded, enemies being tortured, or anything else that suits your fancy. Of course, these shows have no effect on Americans because they know it has nothing to do with them.

"What should I wear?"

American fashions this year are all modeled after the Bonnie and Clyde look, and everyone wants to dress like a gangster. This trend is tongue in cheek, because everyone knows we don't admire gangsters, even though we all consider Bonnie and Clyde a gas.

"What can I buy in the United States that I can't buy in my own country?"

Guns, for one thing. We have no laws about buying guns. You don't even have to go to a store. You can order them by mail from newspapers and magazines.

You can buy shotguns, rifles, handguns, pistols, revolvers, and practically any kind of weapon you want. Of course, we use guns in the United States only for hunting. That's why the American Congress in its infinite wisdom won't pass any gun control laws. They know anyone who would order a gun by mail or buy one in a store would never use it except to shoot game.

"What about visiting American cities?"

It's perfectly safe to visit any American city in the country, provided you don't go out after dark or during certain parts of the day. The best thing is to ask your hotel clerk at the desk. He'll indicate what streets are safe and when you can visit them. Americans pride themselves on law and order and would never do anything to disturb the peace.

"When is the best time to come?"

Any time is a good time to visit the United States, with the possible exception of the long hot summer which starts in the middle of March and goes through October. At this time people are irritable and not as friendly toward tourists as they might be at Christmastime.

"Where can I see the President?"

You can see the White House, but the President, for security reasons, doesn't make many public appearances anymore—at least none that is announced in advance. No other American officials are free to travel either. But as a tourist, this shouldn't bother you. After all, you have a foreign passport.

I hope this answers most of your questions. So forget your cares, and see Americans at work and at play. Watch a truly civilized democracy in action, and meet a people who love one another and live in harmony.

See for yourself why the United States is the leader of the free world and an example to everyone of what you can do when you have understanding, wealth and power.

Visit the U.S.A.

CODDLING VICTIMS OF CRIME

There is so much talk about crime in the streets and the rights of the criminal that little attention is being paid to the victims of crime. But there is a current of opinon that our courts are being too soft on the victims, and many of them are going unpunished for allowing a crime to be committed against them. One man who feels strongly about this is Professor Heinrich Applebaum, a criminologist who feels that unless the police start cracking down on the victims of criminal acts, the crime rate in this country will continue to rise.

"The people who are responsible for crime in this country are the victims. If they didn't allow themselves to be robbed, the problem of crime in this country would be solved," Applebaum said.

"That makes sense, Professor. Why do you think the courts are soft on victims of crimes?"

"We're living in a permissive society, and anything goes," Applebaum replied. "Victims of crimes don't seem to be concerned about the consequences of their acts. They walk down a street after dark, or they display jewelry in their store windows, or they have their cash registers right out where everyone can see them. They seem to think that they can do this in the United States and get away with it."

"They should know better," I said.

"Look at the way we pamper the victims of crime in this country. As soon as they're hit over the head, we call an ambulance and take them to a hospital. If they've got Blue Cross or a hospital insurance plan, most of their bills will be paid. They know they'll get workmen's compensation while they're recovering. What have they got to lose by becoming victims of a crime?"

"You speak as if all the legal machinery in this country were weighted in favor of the victim, instead of the person who committed the crime."

"It is," Applebaum said. "While everyone is worried about the victim, the poor criminal is dragged down to the police station, booked, and arraigned, and if he's lucky, he'll be let out on bail. He may lose his job if his boss hears about it, and there is even a chance that if he has a police record, it may prejudice the judge when he's sentenced."

"I guess in this country, people always feel sorrier for the victim than they do for the person who committed the crime."

"You can say that again. Do you know that in some states they are even compensating victims of crimes?"

"It's hard to believe," I said.

"Well, it's true. The do-gooders and the bleeding hearts all feel that victims of crimes are misunderstood, and if they were treated better, they would stop being victims. But the statistics don't bear this out. The easier you are on the victims, the higher the crime rate becomes."

"What is the solution, Professor?"

"I say throw the book at anybody who's been robbed. They knew what they were getting into when they decided to be robbed, and they should pay the penalty for it. Once a person has been a victim of crime and realizes he can't get away with it, the chances of his becoming a victim again will be slim."

"Why do people want to become victims of crime, Professor?"

"Who knows? They're probably looking for thrills. Boredom plays a part, but I would think the biggest factor is that victims think they can still walk around the streets of their cities and get away with it. Once they learn they can't, you'll see a big drop in crime statistics."

"You make a lot of sense, Professor. Do you believe the American people are ready to listen to you?"

"They'd better be, because the criminal element is getting pretty fed up with all the permissive coddling of victims that is going on in this country."

9

Eyeball To Eyeball

A WONDERFUL COMMAND AFTER
THE PUEBLO

"Commander, we've got a wonderful assignment for you."

"Yes, sir. What is it?"

"The Navy wants you to take command of a ship, sail it up the Yangtze River, and take mud samples and depth readings of the riverbed. We'll give you the latest top-secret equipment for the job."

"That's great, sir. What kind of ship will I have to do this with?"

"We're converting a sardine trawler into a man-of-war. It will be a top-class ship that anyone would be proud to command."

"What kind of guns will she have, Admiral?"

"What do you mean, guns?"

"If I'm sailing up the Yangtze, shouldn't I have some guns on the ship in case anybody wanted to attack me?"

"Why would anyone want to attack you?"

"No reason that I can think of. I just thought if it was a Navy ship, it should have some guns on it."

"The Navy doesn't have guns to spare for every ship in the fleet. Besides, it might look provocative if you were carrying all that secret equipment and guns, too."

"But suppose I'm attacked?"

"Why would anyone want to attack you? After all, you're only looking for mud samples. Look, Commander, if you don't want the assignment, we can always find somebody else."

"Oh, I want the assignment, sir. I just wanted to be clear about what I was to do."

"Well, we've got the whole thing worked out. You sail up to Shanghai from Formosa, make a sharp left, and head straight for Nanking."

"That's the entire plan?"

"Why, what else do you have to know?"

"I'm not trying to make waves, Admiral, but there

183

could be some resistance on the part of the Chinese to my sailing up the Yangtze, even if it's for mud samples."

"The Chinese would never dare attack a U.S. naval vessel. If they did, they know we'd retaliate immediately."

"That brings me to another question, sir. In case I am challenged, will I get aid from any naval vessels?"

"Of course. The Sixth Fleet will be available to give you full protection."

"But the Sixth Fleet is stationed in the Mediterranean."

"I know where the Sixth Fleet is stationed. We can't give you cover from the Seventh Fleet because it's involved in Vietnam; the Pacific fleet at Pearl Harbor will be on maneuvers. So the only ones available for contingency are ships from the Mediterranean fleet. You may have to hold off your attackers until they get there."

"With what, sir?"

"We're issuing all the officers sabers, and the enlisted men will have cutlasses."

"That's different then, sir. I thought we were going in unarmed."

"If anything happens, Commander, all you have to do is give me a ting-a-ling and we'll be there."

"It's good to know I can count on you, Admiral. Sir, I know this is probably a stupid question, but is there any way I can scuttle the ship in case you can't get to me in time?"

"Why would you want to scuttle a good Navy ship?"

"So they wouldn't get all the secret mud-sampling equipment on board."

"Let's cross that bridge when we come to it. The next thing you'll be asking me is what are you supposed to do if you're captured. Ho, ho, ho; ha, ha, ha; ho, ho. That would be a good one, wouldn't it?

"Commander, you're not laughing."

THE MAN WHO GAVE UP SMOKING

Many people have given up smoking since all the bad publicity, and in the majority of cases I admire them for it. But occasionally there is an exception.

I'm thinking now of my friend, De Vries, as an example. De Vries was a "two-pack-a-day" man, and he was very upset about it. He finally decided to quit, and at lunch one day he said he wanted me to be the first to know. "I can do without it," De Vries said. "All it takes is willpower."

I wished him well.

A week later I saw him and asked him how it was going. "I haven't had a cigarette in seven days," he said proudly.

"Bless you," I said. "Your wife must be very proud of you."

"I wouldn't know," De Vries said.

"Why not?"

"I moved out of the house three days ago. And I want to tell you something. I don't miss it at all. What a rat race! She was screaming all the time; the kids were driving me nuts; no one would listen to anything I had to say. Maybe I shouldn't have slugged her, but—"

"You slugged her?" I said.

"Well, it was just a tap. Believe you me, it's been building up for a long time. I mean—I'm amazed I didn't do it before."

I was very disturbed by the news, but I went about my business. I didn't see De Vries again for ten days. Then I ran into him on the street.

"Hey," he said. "You know, I haven't had a cigarette in seventeen days. I don't even miss it."

"That's great," I replied. "How are things going at the office?"

"What office?" he asked.

"Where you work!"

"Heck, I quit four days ago. I was sick and tired of putting up with all the stuff they were handing out. They blamed me for losing the Waring account."

"But you had the Waring account."

"I did until Waring started giving me all the flack about not returning his calls. I told him I had other accounts besides his, and I'd get to his calls when I was good and ready. Boy, did he scream to the old man about that. So I told the old man he had to choose between me or Waring."

"That's terrible."

"Who cares? Ever since I gave up smoking, my tennis game is great, and I've been out on the court every day."

I guess I didn't see De Vries for a month. Then he

turned up at the house one day. "Well," he said, "I haven't had a cigarette in forty-seven days. I'm adding years on to my life."

"Swell. What can I do for you?"

"That's a patronizing thing to say. You act as if I were going to hit you up for a loan. Well, I was, but forget it. You're like everyone else, mean and rotten and spiteful and a bore. I have a good mind to punch you in the nose."

"De Vries, I don't know how to say this to you, but as a friend, I think I should. *Go back to smoking.* There are some people who should give it up and some people who shouldn't. It's nothing to be ashamed of. Besides, you've proved *you can* give it up, and that's the main thing."

My little sermon worked. De Vries is now back with his family, he has a new job where he's doing quite well, we're friends again, and the last time I saw him he said to me, happily, "I don't know how to thank you. Did you know I'm back to two packs of cigarettes a day?"

JACKIE'S BIG MISTAKE

Of all the events of 1968, none had more of an effect on the American people than the marriage of Jackie Kennedy to Greek zillionaire Aristotle Onassis. People who had no opinion on the Vietnam War, the crisis of the cities, or the youth revolution all had something to say about Mrs. Kennedy's nuptials.

It seems to me that what Jackie Kennedy didn't realize was that she was the property of the American people and, therefore, that she had no right to choose a husband on her own. If Mrs. Kennedy wanted to get married again, she should have informed the American public of this, on either the *Johnny Carson Show* or the *Bell Telephone Hour*, and let the American people choose a husband for her.

Once she made her intentions known, special Republican and Democratic conventions would have been called, and candidates would have been nominated for her to marry.

After the nominations, each candidate would have campaigned for Jackie's hand. They would have explained what they would do for Jackie as a husband, where they would live, and how they would raise Jackie's children.

The candidates would have bought television time to let the public know where they stood, not only on the marriage, but also on the public issues of the day.

They also would have traveled across the nation so that Americans could see them in the flesh and decide for themselves which candidate would be the best mate for the former First Lady.

Not only would the public have listened to the platforms of the men it thought were suitable for Jackie's hand, but people would also have decided the complicated questions of religion, age, and nationality of the husband-to-be.

Since they had so much at stake, the public would have taken far more interest in this campaign than they take in the Presidential election.

The climax of the race for Jackie's husband would have been a nationally televised debate between the candidates, so the electorate could see for itself how each man would behave under pressure.

Finally, on election day, Americans from all walks of life would have gone to the polls and voted for the person they wanted to stand at Jackie's side.

In case neither candidate got a majority of the electoral votes, then the House of Representatives would have chosen the man privileged to be Jackie Kennedy's husband.

Once the majority of the American people had made their decision, we all would have abided by it, with no one complaining that he didn't have a vote in Mrs. Kennedy's marital affairs.

This would have been the American way of doing things. Perhaps Mr. Onassis might have won the election; perhaps he might not. But at least the election would have prevented the confusion and despair now rampant in the United States over the Kennedy-Onassis wedding.

Even those who are on Jackie's side admit that it wasn't whom she married, but the way she did it, that has caused so much concern in this country.

No woman of Mrs. Kennedy's stature has a right to decide affairs of the heart by herself. Her marriage was everybody's business, and the least she could have done was poll the American public before she made a decision that affects the lives and pocketbooks of us all.

BEST STORIES OF THE YEAR

It is our pleasure to print the best news stories of the year. These are not necessarily headline stories which you may have read, but rather news items that were buried in the back pages of your paper which you probably missed.

WAILING WALL, California, March 16—Students at Wailing Wall State College marched on the administration yesterday afternoon, yelling for the resignation of Chancellor Winthrop Coldwater and closing down of the school. After breaking windows and scuffling with the police, the students demanded to see Coldwater. When the chancellor appeared, he grabbed the microphone and said, "You should be ashamed of yourselves. I have a good mind to cancel the spring prom."

The shocked students couldn't believe their ears. They publicly apologized to the chancellor for their behavior and immediately returned to their classes.

CHICAGO, Illinois, August 27—Charles McPherson was arrested for wearing nothing but a Vietcong flag on Michigan Avenue last night. At a preliminary hearing before a magistrate, McPherson said that he had assaulted the arresting officer for no reason, and he wished to compliment the Chicago police force on the way they handled his arrest. He also wanted to cite the officer's superiors for their kind treatment and concern when he was booked at the station house. "Something like this," said McPherson, shaking hands with the police, "could only happen in Chicago."

WASHINGTON, D.C., September 1—Pentagon officials testifying before the Senate Armed Services Committee said today that they had all the money they needed for defense purposes and would probably need no more funds for the next fiscal year. A general with the Joint Chiefs of Staff told the Senators, "We've got all the appropriations we can handle now, and it would be foolish to spend more money on new weapons which probably won't work anyway."

MIAMI, Florida, October 12—A Boeing 707 on its way from New York to Miami reported that a dark, bearded man forced his way into the cockpit of the plane. "I suppose you want to go to Cuba?" the captain asked.

"Heck no," the man replied, "they oversold the plane, and they said I could sit up here with you guys."

ATLANTA, Georgia, October 28—William Washington, the first Negro admitted to the Atlanta Athletic Club, resigned today. Asked if his resignation had anything to do with prejudice against him, Washington said, "No. I resigned because they were letting women in the club's dining room at lunch time."

HOLLYWOOD, California, November 12—Sam Shlatzberg announced today that in spite of the new motion picture code he was planning to go ahead with his new film *The Girl Next Door*.

"My story is about a boy who falls in love with the girl next door, and both their families approve. So they get married in a church and have children. I don't give a damn if they give me the seal or not. This is a picture that has to be made."

PARIS, France, December 29—President Charles de Gaulle at his annual press conference told reporters that France had made many mistakes in the past year, and most of them were his fault. He said if he had to do it all over, he would have listened to the United States.

"France," he said, "deserves better leadership. Our problems are too complicated to be resolved by one man."

GETTING LOMBARDI TO COME TO D.C.

The biggest news to hit Washington since Secretary of State Seward bought Alaska for two cents an acre was that Vince Lombardi, former coach of the Green Bay Packers, was coming here to take over the coaching of the Washington Redskins. For those who don't know anything about professional football, the significance of this move is comparable only to Charles de Gaulle's leaving France to become President of Yemen.

Lawyer Edward Bennet Williams, who is president of the Washington Redskins, was so desperate to get Mr. Lombardi after a disastrous Redskin season that he decided to let nothing stand in his way. Lombardi, who doesn't look like De Gaulle, but has a reputation for acting like him, came to Washington to discuss the deal, and this is what happened:

Mr. Lombardi and Mr. Williams were driving down Pennsylvania Avenue, and Lombardi said, "If I come here, I have to have housing."

"Anything you want, Vince," Williams said. "Where do you want to live?"

"What's the matter with that house over there?" Lombardi said, pointing at 1600 Pennsylvania Ave.

Williams gulped. "You want it? You got it."

"OK," said Lombardi. "Now what about getting my stuff moved from Green Bay to Washington?"

"I'll get Air Force One to move you," Williams said.

"I need an office," Lombardi said, "but I like to work in an oval room."

"I know of one," Williams assured him.

"I hear there's a lot of crime in Washington."

"Don't worry about that," Williams said. "I'll get the Secret Service to watch you night and day."

"Now, what about churches?" Lombardi asked. "I like to go to church on Sunday."

"You don't have to," said Williams. "We'll get Billy Graham to come to *your* house."

Lombardi nodded his head. "What about entertainment? Mrs. Lombardi and I like music."

"The Marine Band will come over any evening you want them," Williams assured him.

Lombardi said, "It sounds as good as Green Bay."

Williams pressed his advantage. "If you want to get away, we got a place called Camp David. You call for the helicopter, and you're there in twenty minutes."

"How about getting around Washington?"

Williams said, "Would you believe a bulletproof bubbletop limousine?"

"I must say," Lombardi commented, "you Redskins go first-class. What do I do in the off-season?"

"Would you like to be Chief Justice of the Supreme Court?" Williams said.

"Why not?" Lombardi said. "If I can coach eleven men, I can coach eight."

Later that day I called Williams up. "Did you get Lombardi to come to Washington?"

"Yeh," said Williams nervously. "Now I've got only one more problem."

"What's that?"

"How do I break the news to Mr. Nixon?"

WHEN IS THE SEASON OVER?

I know people aren't going to believe this, but my wife thought that the 1968 football season was over just because it was 1969. This shows how out of touch some American women are.

One Saturday, for example, I was watching a postseason game from Nome, Alaska, brought in by satellite, when my wife came in the room and said, "I thought the football season officially ended on New Year's Day."

"It's true the official college season ended on New Year's Day with the postseason bowl games, but there are still a lot of *post*-postseason games that have to be played."

"*Have* to be played?" she asked.

"Of course. For example, there has to be a game between the Northeastern All-Stars and the Southwestern All-Stars at Sandy Hook, Long Island."

"What for?"

"That's a stupid question," I said. "To play the winner of the Southeastern All-Stars and Northwestern All-Stars game in Cheyenne, Wyoming."

"And what will that decide, that the Rose Bowl, Orange Bowl, Cotton Bowl, and Sugar Bowl haven't decided already?" she asked.

"It will decide what teams will play against each other on Lincoln's Birthday in Springfield, Illinois."

My wife leaned on her broom. "Don't get me wrong. I enjoy football as much as any wife who lives alone, but it seems to me that the 1968 football season should end in 1968, for neatness if nothing else."

"You can't end the 1968 football season in 1968," I said angrily. "There are still too many games that have to be played."

"For example?" she asked.

"Well, you have the Blue and Gray game between the North and the South, and then you have the Red and the White game, between Anglo-Saxons and those of Indian blood. Then there is the Black Power All-Stars against the Uncle Toms, and I haven't even told you who's playing tomorrow."

"Why don't they let the kids go back to classes after they've finished playing football for the season?"

"Because this way the kids get a chance to visit Mobile, Alabama, and Death Valley and Sutter's Creek—places they'd never see if they didn't play football. Don't you understand? Behind every football team in the United States there's a promoter ready to hold a bowl game once the season is over."

"Well, it seems to me they take advantage of those boys."

"Now you're talking like a do-gooder. You have to toughen these kids up if they're ever going to play pro ball."

"Don't tell me the professional football season isn't over either?"

"It's hardly beginning. Haven't you ever heard of the Super Bowl?"

"I know you'll hate me if I say I haven't."

"Well, there's the Super Bowl, and there is the East-West Pro Bowl, and then there's the Runner-Up Bowl, and there's the Coaches' All-Star Bowl, not to mention a special Midnight Bowl, which is going to be played in South Korea as part of Armed Forces Week festivities."

"Could you give me a guess, a wild guess if you like, when the last whistle of the last game of 1968 officially will be blown?"

I took out a pencil and started calculating. Finally I said, "Taking in everying, including postseason, all-star, all-pro, all-coaches, high school, college, and professional football, I would say that the 1968 football season will officially end on June sixteenth, 1969."

My wife sighed. "It seems like only yesterday when they didn't even know if O.J. Simpson would make the *Women's Wear Daily* all-American team."

EYEBALL TO EYEBALL

The most valuable television football watcher's award was presented recently to Harry Dalinsky of Georgetown at a dinner given at Duke Zeibert's restaurant in Washington. Dalinsky, who could not attend because he was watching the Orange Bowl game at the time, was represented by his wife, Marion, who said in her acceptance speech that Harry considered it a great honor to be voted the trophy, which consisted of a silver tray which was a replica of a TV dinner.

Marion, who addressed the 1,200 distinguished guests—all wives of men who also were unable to attend the dinner because they, too, were watching the Orange Bowl game—said, "This is probably one of the great moments in Harry's life, and he told me during a commercial, just before I was leaving for the dinner, that he wanted all of you to know that if he could have possibly got out of his chair, he would have been here tonight.

"Harry wanted to say that this trophy belongs not only to him but to all the people who made it possible—Robert Sarnoff of NBC, William Paley of CBS, Leonard Goldenson of ABC, and the announcers, the cameramen, the technicians, down to the lowliest sound men who gave so much of their time and effort to make him look good."

In presenting the award, Mrs. Robert Yoakum, standing in for her husband, who was supposed to be master of ceremonies, said that Dalinsky had not missed one football game that was televised that year including all the preseason contests, as well as reruns of games from former years.

His eyeballs had covered more yardage and he had passed up more meals and caught more hell from his family than any football watcher of the year.

Mrs. Yoakum said that Dalinsky had received 34,578 votes. The runner-up for the trophy was Gordon Manning of New Canaan, Connecticut, who had been the league's leading watcher until late into November, when unfortunately his house burned down. By the time the fire was out, Manning was able to catch only the last half of the New York Giants-Minnesota Vikings game, and he never was able to regain his stride.

The highlight of the evening were films of Dalinsky watching some of the great football plays of the year. One was of Dalinsky sitting on the edge of his chair as Chicago's Gale Sayers ran a 100-yard kick return. Another showed Dalinsky drinking a beer as the Los Angeles Rams' Fearsome Foursome smeared Baltimore's Johnny Unitas, and a third historical shot showed Dalinsky on his feet changing channels to watch the New York Jets' Joe Namath pass for a 60-yard touchdown play.

One film, shot by director Andy Warhol, showed Dalinsky sitting staring at his set for three hours without moving a muscle. It is considered one of the greatest underground films ever made.

Mrs. Tony Bradley, whose husband was chairman of the awards committee, wound up the evening by saying, "The most valuable television football watcher's award is given to a person, not only because of his viewing ability in the living room, but because he exemplifies the spirit and traditions of the American husband who eyeball to eyeball has devoted his life to watching football on TV.

"It is the Harry Dalinskys of this world who have made TV football viewing what it is today—and an inspiration to the youth of the country, who someday will be watching football themselves."

After the dinner, reporters found Mrs. Dalinsky sitting at a table all alone. When asked what she was doing there, she replied, "Harry told me not to come home until the Orange Bowl game was over."

CONFESSIONS OF A ROOF SELLER

Everyone has a skeleton in his closet that he lives in deathly fear a *Time* magazine researcher may uncover. My skeleton is that I used to sell roofs in Los Angeles. Now I know this doesn't sound like something I should be ashamed of, but that's because nobody really knows the roofing situation in Los Angeles, or at least how it was in the days when I was in the business. I'm sure now it's all different and very much aboveboard.

My life as a roofing salesman began one warm day in 1946, when, as a student at the University of Southern California, I was hitchhiking along Vermont Avenue and was picked up by a man who introduced himself as Johnny B.

Johnny asked me if I was interested in making extra money, and I said it was possible. He told me he was in the roofing business, and he needed a young, clean-cut-looking fellow like myself to act as a legman for him.

I said I didn't know anything about roofs, and Johnny said it didn't matter. He then gave me a fast course in roofmanship.

"The war is over, and everyone needs a new roof," Johnny said. "But if you just go out and ask people if they want a new roof, they're bound to say no. So you have to have a story they're willing to listen to."

"What's the story?" I asked.

"The story is that you are a representative of the Rumraw and Zingoff advertising agency. You are looking for a home in the neighborhood to put on a new asbestos-type shingle. If the homeowner will permit you to put this new roof on, your agency will photograph it, advertise it, and bring around people to look at it. In exchange for any inconvenience caused to the homeowner by all the publicity, Rumraw and Zingoff will arrange to have the roof put on at absolute rockbottom wholesale cost."

"Which," I said brightly, "is probably the same price that any roof would cost."

"You catch on fast for a college kid," Johnny B. said. "Now I don't want you to think we're doing anything dishonest. The people do get a good roof, and besides, they have something to tell the neighbors. It gives them status on their street."

"What am I supposed to do?"

"You give your story to the wife and the husband. If they are *both* interested, you tell them your advertising manager will come by and talk to them, and you set up an appointment. Then I go in with the sales pitch. If they buy a roof, you get ten percent on the sale."

"It sounds easy," I admitted.

The next afternoon I was out ringing doorbells in Los Angeles. It took a week before I made a sale, but the commission was $30, and when Johnny paid me, I was so excited I decided I might make the roofing business my lifework.

My job was quite simple, and I didn't have too much trouble getting someone to listen to my story. I discovered Los Angeles is made up of a lot of lonely people, and they're delighted to have their day interrupted by anybody who has an interesting tale to tell.

I remember once I rang a doorbell and a man answered the door with a fiddle in his hand. He asked me to come in. There was no furniture in the house except for several wooden grocery crates. He told me to sit down, and then he proceeded to play the fiddle. He played for two straight hours without stopping, and every time I attempted to leave, he became very agitated.

Another time a large-bosomed blond lady listened to me make my pitch, and then she said, "What does your advertising manager look like?"

I described him, and she said, "Send him over tonight around eight o'clock."

"Will your husband be home?"

"I'm divorced," she said.

I told Johnny the story, and he said he'd look into it, just on the off-chance that the lady really did want a roof.

The next day I called. "Did you make a sale?"

"What are you talking about?" Johnny wanted to know.

"Didn't she want a roof?"

"Damn," said Johnny, "I knew there was something I wanted to ask her."

Being my age and involved in the type of work I was doing, I must say I was always looking for an "adventure" similar to those all the other salesmen seemed to claim they were having.

There was one fellow—a short, squat, fat, greasy man—whom I used to go out doorbell ringing with at times. He worked one side of the street and I worked the other.

It never failed that sooner or later he would disappear into a house and I'd have to wait an hour for him on the corner. When he finally came out he had a big grin on his face.

"Tell me everything that happened," I'd say excitedly, and for the next two hours, while I gnashed my teeth, he went into every detail about the conquest.

"Why doesn't it ever happen to me?" I cried.

"Your trouble, boy," he said softly, "is all you really want to do is sell roofs."

Johnny B. was fantastic when he went into his sales pitch, and it was rare that he would fluff a sale after I got him into the house.

I went with him on several occasions just to see the master at work.

He walked in with a blowtorch, a beautiful presentation of photographs in a leather-bound, looseleaf folder, samples of the shingle, and, of course, the contract.

Johnny never behaved like a salesman. He always acted as if he were the city health inspector and he were just about to give the homeowners a summons.

He never talked about the roof. He started off by demanding background on the wife and husband. He pointed out his agency had to make absolutely sure that they were upstanding citizens of good moral character. He demanded to know how much money they made, what books they read, whom their children played with. Johnny would find some fault with the construction of the house which made it look as though there were no chance of the agency using the home for display purposes.

In less than an hour both husband and wife were pleading with Johnny to put a roof on the house, no matter what it cost. As a clincher Johnny always asked the people if they had a Bible in the house. They usually did. He then told the couple to place their hands on it and swear to him that neither one had lied to him.

Johnny was beautiful and could have been one of the great actors of our time, if he hadn't discovered early in life there was so much more money in selling roofs.

Occasionally after a roof was put on a house, someone would call in and complain that all the publicity and advertising that they were promised never came to them.

I remember once when I was sitting in the roofing contractor's office on a Saturday afternoon and a call came in. The lady told the boss he had promised to photograph her house and he never had.

"We'll do it this afternoon."

The boss tossed me a Brownie camera and said, "Go out to the house and take some pictures of her damn roof."

"There's no film in the camera," I said.

"Get out of here," he snarled.

I went out and for more than an hour pretended I was taking photos of the lady's roof.

I retired from the roofing business when Johnny decided to expand into barbecue pits. There seemed to be some moral justification in conning someone into a roof, but it was hard to feel I was doing the right thing when it came to barbecue pits, particularly since many of the people Johnny was selling barbecue pits to could hardly pay for their roofs.

It was more than twenty years ago, but every time I fly into Los Angeles, I look down over the roofs trying to see if the ones I sold are still in good condition. And you know something? Despite Johnny and our crooked sales pitch, a lot of them are.

UNHAPPY WIVES

The football season has opened on schedule, and once again families all over the country are being torn apart by the heavy schedule of televised games. I frankly regret the season has come. My wife and I were just getting a good relationship going, and now we probably won't see each other until January.

The last time I talked to her, which was a half hour before the Washington Redskins-Chicago Bears game, I believe she was crying. I remember it quite distinctly because Frank Gifford was showing some great movies of Gale Sayers, and I noticed out of the corner of my eye that my wife was getting tears all over my potato chips.

"I hate soggy potato chips," I said.

But she didn't want to listen to reason. "Why does it have to happen to us every fall? What have I done wrong?"

There was a commercial on, so I put my arms around her. "You haven't done anything wrong, luv. Matter of fact, I was just telling the boys yesterday during half time between the Tennessee-Georgia game, you're a precious jewel, and next to football on TV, I love you more than anything else in the world."

She pushed me away. "I thought so. Well, do you know what I think of football?"

"Don't say something you'll be sorry for," I warned.

"I think it's the great American homosexual game of tag."

"Now you've done it," I said angrily. "Now you've really done it. By making that uncalled-for outburst, you have probably ruined my Sunday afternoon. If I could get up from this chair, I'd probably walk out of this house."

She started crying again, so I moved the potato chips away. "I don't know if I can take another season of this," she said. "It isn't just the Saturday and Sunday afternoons. It's the long, lonely nights when they're showing games, and the game replays in the mornings, and the specials on Vince Lombardi. Don't you have feelings for me?"

"You're exaggerating," I said. "There was no pro football on last Tuesday night. I know that's a fact because it was the night I played poker."

"I'm getting fed up," she cried. "I'm not going to sit here day after day, night after night, wasting away while you make love to a television set."

I was becoming nervous because it was getting near kickoff time. "What are you going to do?"

"I'm leaving. I'm going to find someone who cares about me, someone who wants me for myself." Then she said, "I might even take a lover."

"Hey, that's a good idea," I said. "But will you be sure there's enough beer in the icebox? We ran out last weekend."

She stomped out of the room just in time. Washington had won the toss and had elected to receive.

Ben, Phil, George, Joe, and Doc had shown up by this time. George was the first to notice something was wrong. "These potato chips are very soggy," he said.

"My wife was crying in them," I apologized. "I'll get a fresh bag after the next time out."

"The women are certainly taking the season hard," Ben said. "I never saw them so upset."

"You can say that again," said Doc. "Just before I came over, my wife told me she was going to find herself a lover."

"So did mine," said Phil.

"What did you say?"

"I said she couldn't. I needed the car to come over here."

"None of you seems worried," Ben said.

"Why should we be?" said George. "Who are they going to find when everyone's watching football on television?"

A STARTLING DISCOVERY

Just behind the Pushkin Museum, off the Sixth of March Alley, is a nondescript brownstone which houses the supersecret Soviet espionage organization known as GRUB.

At three o'clock one morning not long ago, a meeting of Soviet leaders was called at the request of Vladimir Kov, the chief of GRUB's infamous American Desk.

Kov opened the meeting by stating that he had just made a discovery which could affect Soviet-American relations for years to come.

"So speak, Kov," said Comrade Kosygin irritably. "It had better be important, to get us out of bed at three o'clock in the morning."

"Comrades," said Kov, "I have startling information that the American male is atrophying!"

"What are you talking about?" Comrade Gromyko shouted.

"Americans are getting smaller. Look at these charts. This is the American male in 1958—and this is the American male in 1968. In ten years his arms have become two inches shorter and his legs three inches shorter."

The Kremlin power structure looked at the charts in amazement.

"What has caused it?" Comrade Brezhnev asked.

"Football," Kov said. "It appears that American men have been watching so much football on television that they are no longer using their limbs. Over a period of time their arms and legs have gotten smaller and smaller."

"Are you sure, Kov?" Comrade Suslov asked.

"Of course I'm sure. These charts were compiled from stolen X rays in more than two hundred American hospitals. Notice that not only are the American male's limbs atrophying, but his spine has been steadily curving from sitting in soft chairs. On the basis of our studies, we predict that in twenty years the average American male will be four feet three inches tall."

Comrade Kosygin shook his head. "But how are we sure that the Americans will continue to shrink?"

"Because there will be more and more football on U.S.

television. In five years there will be six hours of football every night and forty-eight hours on the weekends. It's possible that the American man may never leave his chair in front of the television set, except to get a beer."

Comrade Brezhnev said, "What does this all mean, Kov?"

"It means, comrades, that there is no reason to build an antiballistic missile system. In ten years the Americans will be so small that they will no longer be a threat. Even when attacked, they will refuse to leave their football games."

"And it didn't cost us a kopek," Kosygin said happily.

"But," said Comrade Suslov, "what about the average American woman?"

Kov said, "Because she now has to do all the work around the house while the American man watches television, she is getting larger and stronger. This chart shows that in ten years her arms and legs will have gotten three inches longer."

"This is bad," Comrade Brezhnev said.

"It's good," Kov said. "As American women get larger, their demands on their men become greater, so the men in turn become weaker. If the trend keeps up, by 1978 every man in the United States could become a vegetable."

Comrade Kosygin jumped on the table. "Let's hear it for the Baltimore Colts."

10

The Kremlin Watchers

THE MAN WHO LOST EVERYTHING

The wonderful thing about our neighborhood in Washington, D.C., is that the people rally around when someone is in trouble.

For example, one of our neighbors is McPherson, who happens to own a Silver Shadow Rolls-Royce. It was his proudest possession, but in McPherson's defense it must be said that he never lorded it over the rest of us. Occasionally he might have brought up the Rolls in conversation, but he'd always turn it into a joke such as, "I had a heck of a time parking the chariot this morning," or, "My clock stopped in the Rolls last night, and I had no idea if the motor was running or not." There was nothing offensive in these remarks, but there was no question that the Rolls symbolized everything McPherson had worked for all his life.

While there were a few neighbors who were bored by McPherson's talk about his Silver Shadow, most of the rest of us had a live-and-let-live attitude about it.

Then the roof fell in. It was announced that Rolls-Royce was calling in all its Silver Shadows and Bentley T models because of a possible faulty setscrew in the steering lever.

The first person all of us thought of was McPherson. We tried to phone, but the line was busy. So my wife said, "In a tragedy like this, they'll need food," and she started to make a casserole.

That morning we went over to McPherson's carrying the casserole.

Several neighbors were already there. The minister of the church had also arrived, and when we walked into the living room, he was talking to McPherson:

"The Lord giveth and the Lord taketh away. You have to understand there are overload conditions, even on Rolls-Royces, that no one knows anything about. The mysteries of steering mechanisms are beyond the comprehension of mortal man, but you must believe that there is some master plan beyond all this, and in the long run it will all be for the good."

McPherson, his eyes red, just stared off into space. I went up to him and touched his shoulder.

"I know how you feel," I said sympathetically.

McPherson turned on me. "What do you mean, you know how I feel? None of you knows how I feel. How can I face my friends, my business associates, my golf partners? All my life I dreamed that someday I'd have a Silver Shadow, and now they're taking it away from me."

"Look, McPherson," I said, "it isn't the same as having a Chevy or a Ford or a Chrysler recalled, but all of us have lived through a similar experience. Believe me, in time no one will remember they recalled your Rolls-Royce."

Nolan, another neighbor who was sitting in the living room, said, "Would you like to borrow my Volkswagen while your Rolls is in the shop?"

It was obviously the wrong thing to say because McPherson broke into tears. "Oh, the shame of it. Whoever thought that one day I'd be driving a Volkswagen?"

The minister took McPherson's hand. "Try to imagine that your Silver Shadow has gone off on a trip. Your Rolls-Royce is now in that beautiful, great garage in the sky. And don't forget, you're not losing a car, you're gaining a new steering lever mechanism."

All day long the neighbors came to the house to pay their condolences. Many had baked cakes, others took the McPherson children into their homes, and still others offered to drive the McPhersons anywhere they wanted to go.

By evening McPherson was able to function again, and the first upbeat thing he said was, "Well, I guess there are always taxis."

THEY NEED A COVER STORY

It's hard to believe the Soviet Union would invade a country the size of Czechoslovakia without a decent cover story. Originally, if you recall, the Soviets announced they were coming into the country with other Warsaw Pact troops at the request of Czechoslovak leaders. But someone goofed, because when Russians were asked at the United Nations who the Czech leaders were, the Soviets couldn't come up with one name.

Then the Russians changed their story and said they were invading Czechoslovakia to prevent the Czechs from being overrun by the West Germans. When this one was sent up the flagpole and no one saluted, the Soviets finally said they had invaded Czechoslovakia to protect the Czechs from themselves.

For some reason, the world hasn't bought it, and so the Russians are still hard at work in the Kremlin trying to figure out a story that will justify their occupation.

I have the minutes of the last meeting on the Central Committee in Charge of Invading Small Countries.

"Comrade Petrov, it has been some time now, and we still haven't been able to explain what we're doing in Czechoslovakia."

"I am well aware of that, Comrade Stumpnitch, and I assure you everyone in the fiction division of the Soviet Writers' Union is working on it. As a matter of fact, I have just been given a plan by Boris Bogansky that I wish to submit to the committee."

"Proceed."

"Bogansky suggests we announce that the reason the Soviets invaded Czechoslovakia was to scout the Czech Olympic team for the 1968 Olympics in Mexico City."

"You must be kidding, Petrov."

"I'm not. We should say that the Soviet soldiers manning the tanks are really Soviet track men in disguise, who didn't want to call attention to the real purpose of their visit."

"That's the worst cover story we've heard so far, Petrov, and we've heard some pretty bad ones. Hasn't anyone been able to find one person in Prague who will say he asked us to come into the country?"

"We've found one."

"Great, that's all we need is one. Who is he?"

"The Soviet Ambassador to Czechoslovakia."

"Holy Lenin, what kind of Kremlin do we have, if we can't even come up with a good excuse for invading a lousy little country like Czechoslovakia? What happens when we invade a big country?"

"Comrade Sorovensky, why couldn't we say we went

into Czechoslovakia to prevent an American Zionist Maoist Fascist counterrevolutionary plot?"

"We have said it, you idiot. But no one believes us. Even the Soviet people don't believe us."

"To think there would ever be a credibility gap in the Soviet Union."

"You're all a bunch of stupid hard-line Communists. Here we have six hundred thousand troops sitting in Czechoslovakia, and no one knows what we're doing there."

"Couldn't we say we're there for rest and recreation?"

"No, we can't. Now let's start from the beginning. Why did we send our troops in?"

"To preserve law and order."

"That's not bad. And why did they fire on the population?"

"Because our soldiers were provoked, spit on, cursed, and people threw rotten fish and beer cans on them from hotel windows."

"Of course. And we only used as much force as necessary to restore order."

"That's good. Now what about all the arrests we made?"

"We arrested only those people who, in the opinion of our troops, were disturbing the peace."

"Beautiful, Comrade Rushenko. Where did you get the idea?"

"From watching the Democratic National Convention on television."

A QUESTION OF ROYALTIES

MOSCOW—The Russians do not have to pay royalties on Western works since they have never signed the copyright convention. But if a writer from the West shows up, they will offer to pay him in rubles.

For the past several years, the Soviets have been using my column, and I was told I had thousands of rubles waiting for me. The ruble is valued at $1.11.

My first temptation was to take the rubles and buy caviar with them. But then I saw a vision of J. Edgar Hoover shaking his head angrily and said, "Don't do it, Arthur. You'll become a paid agent of the Communist Party."

I broke into a cold sweat. How could I turn down the rubles without offending the publications that had been stealing my stuff?

I waited for the vision of J. Edgar Hoover to appear again. He came to me a day later, just as I was taking a photograph of the Kremlin palace. "Not the palace, stupid," he said furiously. "Take a picture of the bridge."

"Yes, sir," I said. "By the way, J. Edgar, about those royalties. If I don't accept them, the Soviets are going to get terribly hurt, as well as suspicious. I don't want to blot my notebook with the FBI, but at the same time I don't want the Communists to think I've got that much contempt for money."

An agonized look came over Hoover's vision. "You may have a point. I'll get back to you."

The following day I was in the Pushkin Museum staring at a lovely nude by Renoir. Suddenly the face of the nude was replaced by Hoover's. When my Intourist guide wasn't looking, Hoover whispered, "You know you're being followed, don't you?"

"Of course, I know it," I said. "I'm being followed by a vice-president from the national bank of Kiev. He keeps trying to shove that satchel of rubles in my hands. I can't think of a good reason not to take them."

"Arthur," he said, "you must be strong. Once you take those rubles, you will be in their power and they will use you as they used Klaus Fuchs and Philby."

"I know that," I cried, "but if I refuse the money, they'll think someone else is paying me to write those articles. Couldn't I accept a couple of thousand rubles just for laughs?"

Hoover pursed his lips. "Not one kopek. And don't try anything behind my nude back. I have someone following the man who's following you."

I didn't hear from Hoover for two days. Then, as I was passing a statue of Lenin with his hand pointing out, I saw Hoover's head again in place of Lenin's; "Get a picture of that tank," he said. I looked at where his finger was pointing and snapped a photograph.

"They won't let me leave the country unless I take the rubles," I told him.

"My people have come up with a plan," J. Edgar said. "Call a press conference of Soviet newspapermen and announce that the dollar is in a great deal of trouble and that you're worried it will be devalued at any time. But you know that the ruble will always remain strong. Therefore, you're going to keep the rubles in a bank in the Soviet Union as insurance against the day when the dollar goes to pot."

"That's good thinking, J. Edgar," I said excitedly. "They'll have to buy the story. Thanks so much for helping me out."

"That's my job," he said. "I have to leave now. If you need me, I'll be back in the Renoir at the Pushkin Museum."

AN AMERICAN IN MOSCOW

MOSCOW—The Soviets signed a treaty permitting Pan American Airways to fly to Moscow and Aeroflot, the USSR airline, to fly to the United States. This should open up the gates to tourism for both countries, and no country is better prepared to handle tourists than the Soviet Union.

To add a new thrill to my trip to Moscow, I decided to take an Aeroflot plane. I really didn't decide to take Aeroflot; the Russians decided that for me. I was booked on an Air France plane from Paris to Moscow at nine in the morning. But when I went to get my visa the day before, the Soviet consulate people said the visa wouldn't be ready until ten o'clock, on the day I was leaving.

"But," I protested, "I'm scheduled to leave on Air France at nine."

"You're lucky," the man said. "Aeroflot leaves at noon."

"That's a helluva way to get business for your airline," I complained.

"It's cheaper than advertising," the consulate man shrugged.

I am happy to report that Soviet planes are well constructed and perfectly safe. If there is any flaw in the design of their planes, it is that the aisles aren't wide enough for the stewardesses.

As a safety factor, Aeroflot selects their stewardesses for their strength instead of their looks. That's why you never hear of an Aeroflot plane being hijacked to Havana.

When my wife and I arrived at the airport in Moscow, the Intourist guide who was slated to meet us wasn't there, and there was some confusion about it.

The commissar in charge went through several sheafs of paper, and finally, he said to us coldly, "You were scheduled to come on the Air France flight."

I didn't want to get the consulate employee in Paris in trouble, so I said, "I didn't like the movie they were showing on Air France, and since I knew Aeroflot would be five hours late, it would give me a chance to see the Russian version of *War and Peace*."

This seemed to satisfy him, and he gave me a car and a chauffeur to the Hotel Rossiya, which American newspapermen in Moscow refer to as the Comrade Hilton. The Hotel Rossiya has good beds and is the largest hotel in the world. One lobby overlooks the Kremlin, and the other lobby overlooks the Winter Palace in Leningrad. It is so big and the chances of getting lost are so great that no tourist is permitted to leave his hotel without a canteen of water.

Every problem concerning tourism is handled in Intourist, an all-encompassing state organization which provides cars, interpreters, meal tickets, and free red tape for anyone visiting the Soviet Union.

If you stick to the schedule, Intourist will give you no trouble. But if for some reason you want to change it, you are marked as a petty bourgeois adventurist, and the Intourist people will show you no mercy.

I made the mistake while in Moscow of trying to change my hotel room. The request was granted only after I signed a confession saying that I was working for the CIA and had come to Moscow to photograph the plans of the Hotel Rossiya for a new Holiday Inn that was being built in Chicago.

Despite the language barrier and the problems of coping with Soviet bureaucracy, you can have a wonderful time visiting the Soviet Union.

At the airport just before we were ready to leave, I said to my wife, "You forgot to throw a coin in the fountain at Red Square. Now you may never come back."

She cried all the way to Monte Carlo.

THE KREMLIN WATCHERS

MOSCOW—A diplomatic reception in Moscow has tremendous significance, not only because of the good food and free liquor, but because it is where most foreign observers learn what is going on in the Soviet Union.

I attended a large diplomatic cocktail party at one of the foreign embassies recently, and I was amazed at what the professional Kremlin watchers got out of it.

This is how the conversation went later on in the evening, when everyone was comparing notes:

"Did you notice Golvosky arrived after Kubinsky?"

"That's very interesting, because at the Fourth of July party at the American Embassy Kubinsky arrived after Golvosky."

"And at the Fourteenth of July party at the French Embassy they came together."

"Very significant. By the way, did anyone see Petrov shake hands with Puchinsky?"

"I was going to call that to your attention. It's strange that Petrov should shake hands with Puchinsky when the last time they met, Petrov only nodded at Puchinsky."

"Perhaps Puchinsky's star is rising in the Presidium."

"Or maybe Petrov's star is falling."

"I think we have overlooked the real significance of the handshake. It is not that Petrov shook hands with Puchinsky, but Puchinsky's wife did not talk to Petrov's wife."

"Are you sure?"

"Of course I'm sure. Puchinsky's wife turned her back on Petrov's wife to say hello to Bolgonov's wife. It was a deliberate snub."

"That's very interesting. But to me the most important thing that happened at the reception was that Bolgonov was drunk and spilled vodka all over Marshal Igorvich's uniform."

"What is so important about that?"

"Igorvich was the one who apologized."

"Bolgonov's star must be rising faster than we thought."

"No doubt about it. Marshal Igorvich even went and got Bolgonov another vodka."

"Did Bolgonov spill that vodka on Igorvich's uniform as well?"

"No, but he stepped on the marshal's foot and wouldn't get off it."

"I wonder if this means they're going to make Bolgonov Minister of Defense?"

"He's obviously in for something big. I've never seen Marshal Igorvich allow someone to stand on his foot for so long."

"Did anyone see Zubelkin at the party?"

"You mean the Tashkent poet who was ousted from the Writers' Union for writing a poem attacking the traffic policemen on Gorsky Street?"

"That's the one. He's been rehabilitated and is now permitted to write anything he wants, provided he doesn't ask anyone to publish it."

"The Writers' Union must be going through one of their liberal periods again."

"I don't know if this means anything, but Kavasky spoke to me."

"That is significant because Kavasky never speaks to foreigners. What did he say?"

"I asked him about the Czech problem and he replied, 'I'm sorry, I never speak to foreigners.' "

"Did anyone notice that Gogol spilled vodka on Mutiken?"

"It means nothing. Everyone in Moscow spills vodka on Mutiken. He's become a regular bar rag."

TV IN MOSCOW

You would think that being in Moscow during the Soviet-Czech crisis, I would be very informed about what was going on. But the truth of the matter is I didn't even know there was a Soviet-Czech crisis until I left the country. I blame the Soviet television network for this.

For some reason, which I'll never understand, Soviet TV just isn't doing the job when it comes to informing the public. I know this because I had a television set in my room at the hotel, and I watched it constantly to see if the Soviets were doing any better with their electronics medium than we were doing with ours.

It would be unfair to say Soviet television is better than American television—it's just different.

The first time I turned on the set I hit it lucky. There

was an exciting film on, showing how trucks were assembled in a Soviet factory. Not only did the program feature the trucks being put together by loyal and patriotic workers, but it showed them being greased and tested as well.

This program was followed by a visit to a Soviet stone quarry. For two hours I sat glued to the set watching giant machines tear into a mountain and chew up stones until they were turned into gravel.

During the lull in the program, I decided to change channels (Moscow is supposed to have four), and lo and behold, there was a panel show with a moderator who looked just like David Susskind. Seated around the table were a welder, a dam builder, a woman lumberjack, and the Minister of Canal Barges.

My Russian wasn't good enough to understand what they were saying, but as in America, the fellow who looked like David Susskind was doing all the talking.

I switched to a third channel and got a beautiful test pattern. The fourth channel didn't seem to be working, so I went back to the first channel, where the stone quarry program had just ended. It was followed by a visit to a pipeline workers' congress being held in Byelorussia.

By this time my wife wanted to go sight-seeing, but I was so grabbed by the speeches I told her to wait. She could see the Kremlin any time, but how often could she see a pipeline workers' congress on television?

Two hours later I watched steel being made in a large foundry outside Moscow, and this program was followed by an interview with a professor of Siberian tree transplants. I turned the channel, and the panel was still in session, with the fellow who looked like David Susskind still doing the talking.

My wife kept insisting we leave the room, but I decided to have one more go at the third channel, and I'm glad I did.

Instead of featuring a test pattern, the third channel was now showing a feature film on sheep shearing in Mongolia. Even in black and white it was the highlight of Soviet TV that week.

By this time my wife was getting pretty angry so I reluctantly turned off the set and went out sight-seeing with her. When we got back to the room eight hours later, I immediately turned on the set. Two of the three channels were showing test patterns, but the David Susskind-type panel was still going on, and the guy who looked like David Susskind was still doing the talking.

NO TROUBLE IN RUSSIA

MOSCOW—I hadn't visited the Soviet Union in quite a while, but I am happy to report it is still a workers' paradise and the envy of anyone who is caught up in the rat race of the Western world.

While the West is struggling with its almost insurmountable problems, the Soviets are living in an aura of stability and progress where every day is like the next and one doesn't have to worry about any surprises.

It was my Soviet friend Dmitri who made me realize how far behind the United States was, compared to the Soviet Union.

At lunch he chortled, "I told you the United States would demand to be more like us."

"What on earth do you mean, Dmitri?"

"All your American politicians are screaming for law and order. There is no country in the world that has more law and order than the Soviet Union."

"That's true," I had to admit. "Everyone wants a stronger police force in the United States."

"Forgive me for boasting, but we have more police per capita than anyone. Not only will you find a uniformed policeman on every block, but there are thousands walking around in civilian clothes, and no one knows who they are. It's impossible to be mugged in Moscow."

"How are you fixed on student demonstrations?" I asked.

"We have none unless they're organized by the government, and we have no draft card burners or agitators either."

"This is George Wallace's kind of country," I said.

"When our government officials speak, you don't find anyone picketing them."

"It must be wonderful to live in a land without pickets," I told Dmitri.

"And we don't have strikes."

"American workers never seem to be satisfied," I said. "How do you keep the workers from striking?"

"The governement decides what they should be paid, and the workers agree."

"That certainly is better than collective bargaining."

Dmitri said, "We also have better newspapers than you do. Your newspapers are always criticizing the government and that makes the people unhappy. Our newspapers never criticize the government, so the Soviet people never fret."

"But suppose, heaven forbid," I said, "the government makes a mistake. Who points it out?"

"The government. Otherwise, it's not a mistake."

"I hate to bring this up, Dmitri, but we've been sitting here for hours, and we haven't had any lunch. Is there something wrong?"

"Of course not. Under the Communist system there is no class discrimination in the Soviet Union. A waiter in this country has the same rights as all other citizens, and he is permitted to eat his lunch when we eat ours."

"I see. Then he'll serve us after he's finished?"

"Not necessarily. Since we've done away with the decadent capitalistic system of tipping, a waiter doesn't have to serve us if he doesn't want to. All a Soviet waiter is obliged to do is serve the state."

"Then how does one get something to eat?"

"You tip the waiter before the meal starts," Dmitri said.

"Well, why didn't we do that?"

"I didn't want you to think that was the only way you could get lunch in my country."

11

The Captured
Document Business

VISIT TO A RUMOR FACTORY

While many businesses suffered during the disturbances in our American cities, there was one that thrived—and that was rumor-making. The rumor factories in Washington were going full steam during the crisis, and still they couldn't keep up with the demand.

I visited a rumor factory in the nation's capital recently and was given a tour by the foreman, a jolly, round-faced man named Clarence, who has been manufacturing rumors for thirty years.

"We've been going twenty-four hours a day for the last two weeks, and we've yet to fill all our orders," Clarence said as we walked around the large air-conditioned building.

"I know this is a silly question," I said, "but how do you make a rumor?"

"It's not hard once you get the formula," Clarence told me. "Over here we have the raw facts. Now you mix them with gossip and fantasy, put them through this machine, and they come out a solid rumor. The process doesn't take long, a matter of minutes, but in order for a rumor to have any substance, it has to be kept hot. That's what those burners over there are for. They can heat up a rumor in seconds."

"Where do you get your raw materials?" I asked him.

"Mostly from bars and hairdressers. We have a staff that does nothing but collect bits and pieces of rumor material which they bring in at the end of the day. The ones we don't use right away, we bale and store in a warehouse for later use.

"For example, right now, because of public demand, we've been working on racial rumors, so we've been storing the political tidbits for later on, just before the conventions. Before we switched to racial rumors, we had a big run on Vietnam rumors, but that's died down for the moment."

"How do you distribute your rumors?"

"Distribution is no problem. A lot of them are distributed through taxi drivers, others are dropped off at the press club, some are left on street corners, and, of course, there's always the telephone. During a racial crisis our rumors hardly get out the door before they're grabbed up and spread all over town."

We walked into another room, where several women were inspecting the rumors as they came off the line.

"This is our quality control division. Every rumor that leaves our factory is carefully inspected for holes in it."

"Then you do reject rumors?" I asked.

"We certainly do. A rumor has to withstand tremendous pressure in order to work. If it doesn't hold up, it's not going to be circulated, and pretty soon people will be going to other places to buy their rumors. We've even called in rumors because of a flaw we've discovered in them after they've left the factory."

We walked to another part of the factory, and the foreman said, "This is our research and development division. We're constantly trying to find new methods of making rumors. We had a big breakthrough not long ago. We found out a way of taking old rumors and using them again.

"One of our lab assistants discovered that by taking a rumor circulated in Chicago and doctoring it slightly and fixing it up, it would look like a brand-new rumor for Washington. We're franchising the process for other cities. They'll buy our old racial rumors, and in exchange we'll buy their old rumors. This source of supply will go on forever."

"What happens when you put out a rumor and it turns out to be true?"

"When we let a rumor go, it's a genuine rumor. And there is no truth to it. We have no control over people who will misuse it for their own benefit. As with gun manufacturers, our responsibility stops when our product leaves the factory doors. We can't help it when a hot rumor hits the cold air and becomes a fact."

EVERYONE IS TAKING CREDIT

The most interesting thing about Hanoi's having agreed to talks—any kind of talks—is that both the doves and the hawks maintain they are responsible for Ho Chi Minh's answering the telephone.

A group of doves and hawks were flying around my living room one night not long ago, and each side was claiming victory for its cause.

"I told you the Tet offensive was a victory for our side," a hawk said. "Hanoi is on its knees and that is why it agreed to talks."

"Balderdash," a dove said angrily. "The Tet offensive proved once and for all that we could never win the war in Vietnam, and we'd have to go to the table whether we wanted to or not."

"Fulbright's mustache," another hawk shouted. "Westmoreland said we had the enemy on the run, and they had run out of steam. Hanoi failed to take over the cities and arouse the populace. The Saigon government held the Communists had tremendous losses. The bombing policies finally paid off."

"A pox on the bombing policies," a dove's wife cried. "If we had stopped bombing long ago, Hanoi would have been willing to negotiate then. They said they'd talk if we stopped bombing."

"Aha!" retorted a hawk. "But we didn't stop the bombing. We deescalated the bombing, but we didn't call it off. Yet they still agreed to talk. This proves they couldn't take any more."

My wife said, "Does anyone want any cheese dip?"

A dove ignored her. He addressed himself to the hawks.

"President Johnson finally faced up to the realities of the situation. Unless we wanted to pour in another five hundred thousand men, we wouldn't be able to get anywhere in Vietnam. And even then we wouldn't get anywhere. If it hadn't been for McCarthy and Kennedy, we still would have been bombing Hanoi and Haiphong."

A hawk roared, "McCarthy and Kennedy had nothing to do with the President's decision. He always said he would talk if the other side would talk. Now that the other side has decided to talk, the doves have taken credit for it."

"Why shouldn't we take credit for it?" a dove said. "The military has been misleading the country for four years. If the doves hadn't spoken up, heaven knows where we'd be right now."

"If the doves had shut up," the hawk replied, "Hanoi would never have been encouraged to continue the war."

My wife said plaintively, "The cheese dip is really very good."

"That's a stupid hawk argument," a dove yelled. "Every time we told the truth, we were accused of giving aid and comfort to the enemy. We didn't give aid and comfort to the enemy. The hawks did when they thought they could terrorize Hanoi into coming to the conference table on their knees."

"We never had a chance to use our military power," a hawk said. "If we had been allowed to do what we wanted to do, Hanoi would have damn well sued for peace. It was you nervous Nellies who prevented the military from using everything they had."

"If you don't want the cheese dip," my wife said, "there are some wonderful watercress sandwiches."

"There never was a military solution to Vietnam," a dove said. "There had to be a political solution, and we never could find it."

"So now," said a hawk, "we'll reward Hanoi for her aggression."

"No one is going to be rewarded for anything," the dove said. "We're trying to stop the fighting. Is that a bad thing."

"And what about the domino theory?" the hawk said.

"To hell with the domino theory."

By this time there were feathers all over the living room, and my wife was pleading, "If you don't want the cheese dip and you don't want the watercress sandwiches, will you at least eat cocktail sausages? They won't keep."

THE SUPER-DOOPER AIR BUS IS COMING

"It's coming! It's coming! THE SUPER-DOOPER 400-SEAT JET AIRPLANE—the most luxurious airplane ever to fly the skies."

You've seen the ads in all the magazines, and I'll bet you get the same thrill I do, to know that the air will soon be crowded with large flying buses carrying millions of people up and down, up and down.

Of course, the advertisements don't answer certain questions that come to mind when you see the four-color glossy spreads, so I went out to interview Rudolph Hammilfinger, the designer and engineer of the Super-Dooper sky bus which will eventually carry 567 passengers at one time.

"Mr. Hammilfinger," I said, "you have certainly designed a nice ship, but what worries me is that there isn't an airport in the country that can handle an airplane of that size."

"That isn't my problem," Hammilfinger said angrily. "I just build the airplane. I don't worry about what they do with it once it leaves the factory."

"That's wonderful, sir, but isn't there any thought given to situations that might arise when you are loading and disgorging five hundred and sixty-seven passengers at one time?"

Hammilfinger said, "That's the airline companies' problem. If they didn't order such large planes, we wouldn't make them. I suggest you go talk to an airline company executive and present the question to him."

I went to see Rodney Clover, executive vice-president of Jam-Packed Airlines.

"Mr. Clover," I said, "your company has just ordered fifty Super-Dooper air buses which you intend to put into service next year. How can you handle the passengers on these new enlarged planes?"

"The airports have to worry about that. We're concerned with seeing that more and more people fly. As long as we fill up our planes, we'll be doing our job."

"But don't you conceive that there will be chaos when you put the Super-Dooper air bus into service?"

"There will only be chaos if the airports don't live up to their responsibilities."

I said, "It seems to me that unless you have the ground problems worked out, you shouldn't be flying those big planes."

"We ordered them, we paid for them, and we're going to fly them. The people you ought to speak to are the airport authorities. They're supposed to figure out what to do with the planes when they land."

I immediately went over to the Airport Managers Association to speak to Timothy Merryweather, the spokesman for airport managers. "No one consulted us about the Super-Dooper buses," he said, "so we're not going to take the rap when the whole system breaks down. All we try to do is run a neat airport. You ought to speak to the Federal Aviation Authority. They're supposed to be working on what to do with the big planes."

I went over to the FAA, where a man behind a desk said, "It's Congress that's at fault. If they won't authorize enough funds to build and enlarge airports, they are going to be responsible for causing one of the most disastrous catastrophes in transportation history. Go talk to the Hill."

I dutifully went over to Congress. But as luck would have it, they weren't in session. It was just as well. They probably would have sent me back to Rudolph Hammilfinger.

WHAT TO DO WITH THE MOON

Well, we really've had a close look at the moon, and we know for a fact that man can get there and back. The next question that has to be answered is what do we do with the moon now that it's in our grasp.

A top secret meeting was held in Washington recently to discuss this thorny problem.

General Wilco Andout, the U.S. Air Force representative, said, "I don't think we have anything to discuss. The moon should become our first outer-space Air Force base. We've already drawn up the plans, and for fifty billion dollars we can give the U.S. a superdeterrent that will set the Soviets back on their ears. Even if they knocked out every rocket on earth, we'd still have our hardware on the moon for the final crunch."

Admiral Shipstead of the Navy said, "The moon should be a naval base. After all, it will have to be supplied by spaceships, and we're in charge of all ships."

Army General Trenchfoot said angrily, "If the moon has to be occupied, then it's the infantry's job with Air Force and naval support, of course."

A representative of the Department of Parks spoke up: "I object. I think we should make the moon into a natural park where people can get away from the cares of the world. We should leave it just as it is, only adding a few refreshment stands and places where people can deposit their refuse."

The Department of Transportation jumped in. "Wait a minute. Our highway people have surveyed it, and we believe the thing to do with the moon is to pave it from one end to the other. The only way you're going to get people to go to the moon is to provide them with something to drive on."

The Department of Urban Housing and Development man objected. "The moon should be used for a housing development. My department wants to start a pilot program with private industry. We propose to sell the best views of earth for high-rise apartments and luxury hotels to real estate developers, if they in turn will invest in low-cost housing for the poor on the dark side of the moon. This way the costs of public housing would be kept down."

Health, Education, and Welfare spoke up. "We'll support that program mainly because we'd like to see if busing school children from the earth to the moon would be feasible."

"Wait a minute," said the Department of Agriculture man. "We think the moon should be set aside for farming and grazing."

"You can't grow anything on the moon," someone shouted.

"All the better," the Department of Agriculture man said. "We pay large sums of money to farmers for not growing anything. If we had the moon, we could triple our budget."

Treasury had a man there. "The Secretary insists that nothing be done about the moon until we find out if there is any tax money we can squeeze out of it."

The Department of Commerce spokesman interceded. "I know of seven conglomerates that want to make a bid for the moon, for no other reason than they consider it a growth stock. I have also been approached by several advertising agencies that would like to lease the moon for outdoor advertising purposes. Our agency plans to build the largest neon sign in the universe for its detergent client, and not only won't it cost the government a dime, but they're willing to pay two million dollars to lease the space."

Everybody in the room started to yell at once. Suddenly the head of NASA walked in, white-faced, and gaveled the meeting to order.

"Gentlemen, I have just received word that Howard Hughes is willing to buy the moon at any price."

"What does he want to do with it?" someone shouted.

"Hughes doesn't plan to do anything with it. He says he just wants to buy it as protection against anyone's ruining his view of Las Vegas."

THE CAPTURED DOCUMENT BUSINESS

As everyone is aware, the best source of information concerning how a war is going is captured enemy documents. If it weren't for these captured documents, our political and military leaders in Vietnam would certainly not have been as optimistic about the war as they were.

By chance I came across an enemy document myself, and it was a windfall because it described how the North Vietnamese were managing to get their captured enemy documents into the hands of the South Vietnamese and Americans.

It seems that Hanoi has turned over the responsibility of manufacturing and distributing captured documents to the 101st Captured Enemy Document Brigade. The headquarters of the 101st CED Brigade is located five stories underground somewhere near the Chinese border. There, under the supervision of the notorious Colonel Vinh Su, a Soviet-built mimeograph machine turns out an average of 10,000 enemy documents a day.

Because of wartime conditions, these captured documents are printed on a heavy low-grade paper which is one of the main reasons American intelligence believes that Hanoi is ready to throw in the towel. No country can survive long if it has to print its orders on low-grade paper.

But the paper has a twofold purpose. After the documents are printed, they are issued to North Vietnamese and Vietcong soldiers as part of their uniform. The captured enemy documents are used as insulation for the wet-weather jackets, as well as for stuffing into sandals when the cheap North Vietnamese leather gives out.

It is for this insulation that North Vietnamese soldiers and Vietcong are so anxious to carry captured enemy documents on themselves. The documents are also used as handkerchiefs and for starting fires, though General Vo Nguyen Giap, in a recently captured enemy document, warned his troops that burning a document that could eventually fall into the hands of the Americans was a court-martial offense.

Although all Vietcong forces are issued captured enemy documents, the 101st CED Brigade is solely charged with carrying the highly classified ones which eventually will get to the Pentagon and then be given to pro-administration columnists.

The members of the 101st are given extensive training. They are then sent out on patrol with the captured documents hidden in their knapsacks. As soon as they see a South Vietnamese or American unit they throw up their hands and surrender. While being searched, they babble that they all were innocently duped by the Communists.

Needless to say, there is a big turnover in the 101st Brigade, particularly when its main mission is to be captured. But the supplying of captured enemy documents to Saigon has highest priority for Hanoi, and the demand for them has increased with each new escalation.

As a matter of fact, there is now a black market in captured enemy documents, and many South Vietnamese have decided to manufacture them to sell to the various American intelligence agencies.

These captured documents are printed on better paper and are easier to study since they weren't carried down from the North. Also some enterprising forgers are printing them in English to make them easier for the Americans to read. This has naturally angered the North Vietnamese who have demanded that unless the illicit traffic in captured enemy documents ceases, they will not come to the conference table.

"It's our biggest export item," Colonel Su told a visiting French newspaperman, "and now they even want to take that away from us."

HOSPITALS ARE NEW STATUS SYMBOLS

Hospital rates are rising at such a phenomenal rate that some experts predict it is conceivable in fifteen or twenty years that a room at a good hospital will cost $700 a day.

If this is true, and it's hard to imagine it isn't, going to a hospital will become a status symbol for the very rich only, just as owning a yacht and a stable of horses has been in the past.

Society editors will be assigned to cover hospitals, and this is how a society column might read in the future:

Mrs. William Vanderwhelp of Newport and Sag Point has checked into Doctors' Hospital before going to her winter home in Palm Beach wearing a Courrèges hospital gown especially made for her. Mrs. Vanderwhelp said, "They may criticize me for going to the hospital, but I think if you've got the money and the time, you might as well have the fun that goes with it."

At the same hospital was Reginald Winthrop Clover, heir to the Beanie Breakfast Cereal fortune, who just had his appendix out. Asked what the operation cost, Reggie replied, "To paraphrase J. P. Morgan, if you have to ask what it costs to have an operation, you can't afford one."

Meanwhile, up at Rose Hill Hospital, Mary Lou Astorwood gave birth to a baby boy. Since it was their first child, the Astorwoods took a private room which cost them $10,000 for the week. The proud father, Clyde Astorwood, said, "The Astorwoods have always had their babies in hospitals, delivered by a doctor, and there is no reason for the press to make an issue over it. I think you should be able to spend your inheritance as you darn well please."

There is still a battle raging at the Maple Flower Hospital. It started when the board of directors decided to admit charity patients, who could only afford to pay $500 a day for a bed in the ward. Bart Clogswell, the oil trillionaire, said that by changing its admittance policies, Maple Flower was opening the floodgates to "riffraff," and the peace and harmony of the hospital would be endangered.

Ellen Maloney McMahan, another member of the

board on the other side, said the ward patients would not be permitted to mingle with the other patients because the private and semi-private rooms had been designated as the "clubhouse," and the wards had been designated as the "grandstands."

Liz White Whimple had a gallstone removed at the Lincoln Memorial Hospital Saturday. The operation was performed in the Palladium Room, which had been decorated especially for the occasion. Peter Duchin and his orchestra played during the postoperative surgery, while Meyer Davis' orchestra was hired to play for her after she got back to her room. Liz had special gowns designed for the surgeons and nurses. It was probably the most lavish gallstone operation of the year, and could only be compared with Truman Capote's tonsillectomy of last spring, when Truman rebuilt the operation room amphitheater to look like the Madrid bullfight ring.

Odds and Ends: What doctor is thinking of setting the broken arm on what former debutante who has been married four times? . . . Did Lily Fitzwhistle, the sparkplug heiress, check in secretly at Bonnie University Hospital for slipped disk? . . . The Duchess of Amblemeyer claims she is tired of going to Queen Mother's Hospital in London for her ulcer, and said she would have all her ulcer work done in the future at Arthur's Sanitarium in New York, where most of the beautiful people go. . . . Frank Sinatra was turned away for treatment from Boswell Hospital after a fight the other night because he wasn't wearing a tie. When told by a reporter whom he had turned away, the chief surgeon said, "I don't care if it was Richard Burton himself, the hospital has to maintain a decorum, or we'll lose all our clientele."

Next week I'll tell you about two hernia operations that were planned months in advance on the same day without either playboy knowing it.

A BREAKTHROUGH IN AIR TRAVEL

I am constantly amazed how the airlines are solving their problems. Everyone is aware that one of the big stumbling blocks to future air transportation is airport facilities. No airport in the country is prepared to handle the new air buses carrying 400 passengers that will soon be put into service.

I was under the impression that no one was working on the crisis, but I was wrong. The airlines and airports together are solving the problem in one of the most unconventional ways that human engineers have ever devised.

They're making people walk to their destinations.

As the airports get larger, they keep extending their terminals, and the gates to the aircraft keep getting farther away.

I discovered the consequence of this the other day when I had to catch a plane in Chicago for Davenport, Iowa. I started walking toward my gate; then realizing I had only an hour to make it, I started jogging. A few miles later I discovered I still wasn't anywhere near the gate, so I started sprinting. But because I was carrying a briefcase, I just didn't have the spurt I needed for the last few miles, and I missed my plane.

The airline ticket attendant was very sympathetic and said to me, "Why don't you walk to Davenport? It's only a few more miles down the road."

"Only a few more miles down the road?"

"Yes, we don't like to talk about it, because we naturally want people to fly, but most of our airline terminals have been spreading out so far that our departure gates are located only a few miles from where people are going. If you look out the window, you can see the lights of Davenport right over there."

"That's amazing," I said. "I knew I had gone pretty far, but I didn't think I was anywhere near Davenport."

"Most people don't," the ticket attendant said. "But, you see, we have to keep extending the wings of the terminal to handle the traffic, and so the cities get nearer and nearer. Someday we hope to link the Davenport and Chicago airports so passengers can *walk* between the two of them without getting wet. It certainly will solve the pressing airport traffic problems."

I thought Chicago was the only airport doing this, but not long ago I was out in Los Angeles and had to make a plane for Santa Barbara. When I was given my gate number for the flight, I started for it. And you can imagine my delight and surprise when I discovered that by the time I got there I was only five miles from the Santa Barbara city limits.

Then recently I was in Miami and had to fly to Tampa. As I walked through the terminal to my gate, I stopped off for lunch at the Palm Beach Airport snack bar and then continued straight on to find my plane was parked at a gate number just beyond Orlando.

I found out that every major airport in the country is now working on tunnels and ramps which will eventually hook up with airports in other cities. It's the first breakthrough in airline congestion. Engineers predict that in the not too distant future every airline terminal in the United States will be linked together, and by the time a passenger reaches his gate number on foot he will have arrived at the place where he originally intended to fly.

12

Is The Four-Letter Word Obsolete?

THE DARK DAYS BEFORE PLAYBOY

It's very hard to imagine what America was like before *Playboy* came on the scene. In order to put it in its proper perspective, you have to remember that in those days the United States was an agricultural society and the deep Puritan instincts of its people dominated the land.

A "good" woman neither smoked nor drank, and she stayed at home while her menfolk spent their time in clubs and taverns. A "lady" of the late 1940's and early 1950's didn't go out on a date without a chaperon, who stayed discreetly in the background, but nevertheless was there to prevent any hanky-panky.

Social life for young people was organized around church dances and occasional hayrides, but any kind of necking or outward display of emotion was frowned on and very quickly discouraged.

A "lady" never spoke unless she was spoken to, and she always retired from a room when men entered it, unless she was specifically asked to stay.

The fashion of the time for women was quite strict. Skirts were down to the ankles, corsets were the order of the day, and if a woman showed any part of her "leg" (the word was never used in mixed company), she was considered "loose" and not fit company to be brought home to the family.

I'm sorry to say that there were some "loose" women in the United States in the early fifties. They could be found in restaurants and nightclubs, smoking and drinking until all hours of the morning. But they paid a price for their wild behavior and frivolous conduct. They were scorned by the good people of the town, and it was made known in no uncertain terms that they were not welcome in good society.

Some taboos were breaking down even in the early fifties. "Good" women were permitted to go to the cinema, but only if their fathers or brothers approved of what they saw. Walt Disney was the most popular family type of entertainment, and so of course, was Andy Hardy.

The automobile was just coming into its own, and occasionally you would see one roaring down Main Street in a cloud of dust with everyone screaming after the driver, "Get a horse." But it was considered very bad for a girl from a good family to go driving off with a man alone.

The sexual taboos of the early fifties were numerous and fierce. The word was never discussed in the household. Anything to do with sex was done behind locked doors out of earshot of the children and servants. Premarital sex was unheard of, and the sex act, as we know it today, did not exist. Marriages were consummated solely to have children, and any pleasure derived from it was strictly an unwelcome byproduct. As a matter of fact, in some towns such as New York, Chicago, and San Francisco if a woman experienced anything during intercourse she was considered a nymphomaniac and in need of psychiatric therapy.

Men had it a lot easier during the Puritan fifties. They could go to a bar and pick up a woman to relieve their physical desires. Some women accepted payment in cash, others took gifts, and still others could be seduced after being fed a certain number of drinks. The men of the time were never severely censured for this behavior, provided they didn't brag about their peccadilloes at home.

This was the state of the country in 1952, and America might have stayed that way except for a young man who came on the scene. His name was Hugh Hefner and he was a rugged fighting revolutionary who was fed up with the hypocrisy that was rife in the land. One night in a beer hall in the German part of New York City, Hefner met with a small group of men who thought the way he did. They decided to bring about a sexual revolution in the United States of America, even if it cost them their lives.

They named themselves the Playboy Party, after a free-sex martyr named Eric Playboy who had been kicked out of the FBI for sleeping with his secretary. Hefner felt the best way to take his message to the people was through a magazine, a magazine that would tell the truth about sex and morals and breast feeding. Not only would Hefner use the magazine to liberate Americans sexually, but the profits from it would go toward building clubs all over the country to enlist members in the fight for emancipation.

But before he could get the project under way, an informer from the United States Post Office tipped off the police, and Hefner and his little band were driven from the outskirts of New York. They wandered west from town to town, preaching their gospel of love and love and love, sometimes being jeered, sometimes being stoned, and sometimes getting lucky.

Finally, one morning the little group, hungry and tired, reached a hill overlooking the town of Chicago. Hefner stood on the top of the hill, and as far as he could see there were girls. He turned to his loyal followers and said, "This is the Playce."

Hefner set up his headquarters in a bunker and started turning out his magazine, first by mimeograph, then by offset, and finally by eight color presses.

A dissatisfied and frustrated America was ready for his message, and before anyone knew it women revolted against the system. First they started to smoke, then they started to drink, and finally they decided to go all the way. They stripped themselves of their confining clothes; they turned their backs on organized dances; they took rides in automobiles without chaperons. The Puritanical Reactionary Establishment shook their heads in disbelief as one new freedom led to another. And then someone, Hefner denies it was he, invented a pill, and the last barrier to sexual freedom came tumbling down.

The dark days of the forties and fifties are behind us. Thanks to Hugh Hefner and his dedicated little coterie of free thinkers, sex is now something to be enjoyed by everyone regardless of race, creed, religion, *or* sex.

All of us owe him a debt of gratitude which we will never be able to repay. Hugh would be the last to remind anyone of this debt, but I think one way we could remember him is that the next time we're having an affair, we say to ourselves, "Let's win this one for Hefner."

WARRANTIES I HAVE KNOWN

Betty Furness, in a recent speech, revealed something that the average consumer has known for years. It is that the

warranties that come with most American products aren't
worth the computer cards they're printed on.

There may have been a lot of changes in Washington in
1969, but one thing you can be sure of: the American
consumer is getting a shafting by the great free enterprise
system.

Not long ago I went to McCarthy, Swaine, and
Klutzknowlton, the appliance store, to return an electric
can opener I had bought my wife for Christmas.

"Why do you wish to return it?" the man asked.

"Because it doesn't work."

"Did you fill out the Green Warranty Card that came
with it?"

"Yes, I did."

"And what happened?"

"The can opener still didn't work."

"I see. Could you tell me how soon you filled out the
Green Warranty Card after you got the electric can
opener?"

"Maybe three days, a week. I'm not sure."

"But it specifically says that the Green Warranty Card
must be filled out twenty-four hours after purchasing the
appliance."

"Yes, but since it was a Christmas present, we didn't
open up the package until Christmas morning, and therefore we didn't see the Green Warranty Card and have a
chance to fill it out for a few days as we were too busy
trying to get the thing to work."

"But if you didn't fill out and mail the Green Warranty
Card within twenty-four hours of the purchase, it's hardly
our fault that the electric can opener doesn't work, is it?"

"I wouldn't say that," I said. "I think I should get a new
electric can opener."

"We can't do that. The only one who has the authority
to give you a new electric can opener is our warranty
department, which is located in Leavenworth, Kansas. But
since you didn't send in the Green Warranty Card within
twenty-four hours of purchase, they probably have no
record of your buying an electric can opener in the first
place."

"You have a record of it. Here's my sales slip."

"Yes, that's true. We know you purchased an electric

can opener, and *you* know you purchased an electric can opener, but Leavenworth, Kansas, doesn't know."

"Look," I said, "I should think you would be worried for the good name of McCarthy, Swaine, and Klutzknowlton."

"But we're not owned by McCarthy, Swaine, and Klutzknowlton anymore. We were bought out by Federated Pumps and Warehouses, which is a subsidiary of Drinkwater Fire and Theft, which is owned by Sable Hosiery and TV Antennas, which merged last month with Moon Orbiting Platforms, Inc."

"That's great, but what about a new electric can opener? Just give me one, and I'll be on my way."

"We can't. You see, we've discontinued making electric can openers."

"How could you discontinue making them? I just bought this one for Christmas."

"That's why we discontinued them. A lot of people bought them, and they didn't work. I guess our mistake was putting the head of our tire division in charge of electric can openers."

"What do I do now?"

"I'll take your name and see if there is some way of getting Leavenworth to accept your Green Warranty Card even if it was sent in late."

"And will that get me a can opener?"

"Of course not. But it will put you on our mailing list for any new appliances we plan to put out this year."

INSURANCE IS GOOD FOR YOU

Montgomery Ward and Company came under attack recently for an insurance plan it has instituted for its charge account customers. The insurance automatically covers charge account bills up to $3,000 in case of the death of the person holding the account. The premiums are charged to the customer unless he specifically writes to the company and says he doesn't want it.

What annoyed many customers was that they were paying premiums on a life insurance policy they didn't ask for or know they had.

The only one who wasn't too bothered by the Montgomery Ward insurance ploy was my friend Spritzer, who loves to match wits with some of the largest corporations of this nation.

As soon as Spritzer heard that he was being charged for a life insurance policy he had neither applied for nor wanted, he wrote the powers at Montgomery Ward a letter:

DEAR SIRS,

I understand you have taken out a life insurance policy just in case something happens to me before I make all the payments on my new washing machine. This is good thinking, as you never know when I'm going to pop off and you're going to be stuck with the bill. I think you're wise to worry about me particularly, since with all the aggravation my kids are giving me, I could have a heart attack any day.

But the thought occurred to me, when I heard about *your* insurance policy, that I had no protection in case something happened to Montgomery Ward and Company.

I'm not wishing you any worse luck than you're wishing me, but through the years I notice that Montgomery Ward has had some very big ups and downs and I've started to get a little nervous about what would happen to my washing machine if, God forbid, Montgomery Ward should have a heart attack.

I'm sure it couldn't because I know that at the moment you're in excellent health, but as business people, you must understand I have to prepare for the worst.

If something happened to you, I couldn't very well go to Sears, Roebuck and say, "Hey, would you come out and fix my washing machine?" any more than you could say to my loved ones, "Sorry about Spritzer passing away, but he still owes us money on his appliance."

So I have decided to do the only honorable thing and take out an insurance policy to protect me from Montgomery Ward going out of business. You, of course, will have to pay the premium on it, since I'm taking the big risk by owning one of your appliances. But in order to save you the time and trouble of paying on the policy, I will deduct the premium from my payments on the washing machine.

Unless I hear from you to the contrary, this insurance

policy goes into effect immediately. As long as Montgomery Ward remains in good health, you have nothing to worry about. But if something comes up—and believe me, I'm not predicting trouble—you can rest easy in the knowledge that there will be enough money left over from your estate to take care of my washing machine.

Please understand there is nothing personal in this, and I wish Montgomery Ward a long and happy life, but let's face it, all our destinies are still dependent on that "great retailer in the sky."

Sincerely yours,
SPRITZER

FIRST READ THE INSTRUCTIONS

There are so many different kinds of clothes made of miracle fibers that one is hard put to remember the instructions on how to launder and clean them. Each new piece of clothing now comes with a long list of instructions explaining how the garment must be treated, plus many warnings about what will happen if the instructions aren't adhered to.

One day I came home to find my wife washing my 45 percent alphazate, 25 percent prymnon, 30 percent cotton turtleneck sweater. I was horrified to discover that she was washing it the wrong way. "You're supposed to wash that sweater in cold lamb's milk, and you're washing it in warm lamb's milk."

"No," she said. "I read the instructions quite clearly. You wash it in warm lamb's milk and then you rinse it in cold."

"You're thinking about my hundred percent all-kozel undershirts. My turtleneck sweater is just the opposite."

I was right, because as we were talking, the turtleneck started to disintegrate before my eyes.

"That sweater cost me twelve dollars," I cried.

"I can't keep all these washing instructions straight," she said angrily.

"What are you going to do now?"

"I'm going to wash your eighty-nine and a third percent rogiflex wash-'n'-dry shirt."

"You have to use fresh essence of lime, mixed with distilled underground spring water," I reminded her.

"Are you sure? It seems to me that there was a warning attached to the shirt that if you used distilled underground spring water, the colors would run."

"That applies only to shirts with French cuffs," I told her.

"Of course," she said. "What an idiot I am for not keeping it straight."

I started to put on a clean pair of socks. My large toe went right through the sock.

"What the blazes did you do with my socks?"

"Nothing. I put them in the washing machine, added virgin calf detergent, two tablespoons of chlorine, and a cup of epsom salts, according to the instructions sewn in the sock."

I read the instructions. "Did you set the washing machine at seven and a half revolutions per minute?"

"I tried to, but I had to hold it manually and my arm got tired," she confessed. "I guess at the end the machine was going nine revolutions per minute. But I figured it didn't matter."

I threw down the socks in disgust. "If it didn't matter, why would they sew the instructions into the sock?"

She started to sob. I felt bad and said, "It's all right. I'll buy another pair of socks that can be washed at nine revolutions per minute. Well, I think I'll put on my hundred percent stay-pressed-forever seersucker suit."

I put on the pants. As I was inserting the belt, the legs, just below my hips, collapsed and fell to my ankles.

"What did you do to my suit?" I yelled.

"I had it dry-cleaned."

"You're not supposed to dry-clean a stay-pressed-forever material," I screamed. "Look, it says right here in the coat that the only way to clean it is to place it over an air-conditioning unit for twenty-four hours."

"I put your Nehru suit over the air-conditioning unit."

"The Nehru suit has to be dipped in naphtha and airline hydraulic fuel."

"It didn't say so in the coat."

"The instructions were printed on the beads that came with the suit."

"Don't yell at me," my wife yelled. "If you bought suits

made of wool and shirts made of cotton, you'd have something to wear tonight."

"Yeah, but then look at the laundry and cleaning bills we'd have."

NOT FOR WIVES

Mr. Jack Valenti of the Motion Picture Producers Association has done a fine job with this rating system of films. In order to protect children, his association now informs people through the advertisements and outside the theater whether they are suitable for the whole family or just the adult part of it. The ratings start with G for the family, then go to M for mature audiences, and finally to X where human beings under sixteen are not admitted.

I am not criticizing Mr. Valenti's ratings but actually trying to improve on them. I think he should add another category to warn husbands what to expect. This rating on a film could be X-NFW—which would stand for "not for wives."

I say this because I went to a film the other night with my wife only to discover when we got to the theater that it had an X rating.

"What does that mean?" she wanted to know.

"It means that this picture is an adult film, and only those of us who are mature enough and grown up enough to understand the implications of what the producer and writer and director are trying to say are permitted to see it."

"You mean it's a dirty picture?" she said.

"We must not use the word 'dirty' in describing a film. It is an art picture, aimed at a specific audience who want more out of life than Doris Day and Rock Hudson."

"Those billboards out front look pretty dirty to me."

"What's the matter? Haven't you ever seen a girl tied behind a bulldozer before?"

"Not while it's knocking down a building."

"Well, billboards never really show what the movie is about. It's just a way of getting you into the theater."

"I'd rather see *Oliver*," she said.

"Don't be square. If adults don't support X-rating films, who will?"

Before she could change her mind, I bought the tickets, and we went in.

"The popcorn even looks dirty," my wife said.

"Will you stop behaving like someone who *only* attends movies for the entire family?"

We sat down just behind six members of a motorcycle gang and next to an old man who was reading *Candy* while the lights were on.

Finally, the movie started. It opened up with a woman being whipped by ten members of the Royal Canadian Mounted Police.

"Let's go," my wife said.

"We can't go until we've found out what she's done. Perhaps that's the way people are punished in Canada."

"Nelson Eddy never whipped Jeanette MacDonald."

The scene shifted to a pair of lumberjacks walking through a forest with their arms around each other. They stopped in a clearing.

"That does it," my wife said. "I'm going."

"But there's supposed to be a big scene between two girls from Toronto and three women from French Canada who want independence from the Commonwealth."

She was on her way up the aisle, and I followed her.

"I just want to ask one question," she said as we were driving home. "What was the point of that Mountie kissing his horse?"

"Oh, come on. Haven't you seen a man kiss a horse before?" I said.

"On the lips?"

IS THE FOUR-LETTER WORD OBSOLETE?

The four-letter word, which in the past could only be seen on the walls of men's washrooms and heard only in GI barracks, is now popping up all over the place. This is causing a great deal of concern among philologists who feel that the word is becoming so common that it will soon lose its impact.

Professor Weymouth Langue, who has made a lifetime study of four-letter words at the University of Kussin, told me that unless the trend is reversed, the four-letter word would soon become as obsolete as the five-letter word "Edsel."

"There are only two four-letter words that I am concerned with," said Professor Langue. "While you still can't print them in your newspaper, I'm sure you know which ones I mean. In the past these words had the most powerful effect on the English language. The reason for it is that they were used sparingly and only under very great provocation.

"But, alas, in the last ten years, the words are written into every stage play, and they are included in every best seller. Underground newspapers feature them in headlines, national magazines vie to print them in feature stories on Norman Mailer, and the latest place they've appeared is on the foreheads of students at the antiwar demonstrations in Chicago. There doesn't seem to be any place where one can't hear or read a four-letter word these days."

"And this bothers you?" I asked.

"Only because the words are losing their value. I have always believed that once you had proliferation in the use of these two four-letter words, they would have very little retaliatory effect. For years, they have given tremendous release to people under pressure. I doubt if our GI's could have got through any of their wars without them. But now, through overuse, there is a great deal of apathy when you hear a four-letter word, and it has as much effect on you as the word 'rain' or 'book.' "

"But according to Mayor Daley, one of the reasons the police might have overacted in Chicago was because of the four-letter words used against them by the mobs. They must have some emotional impact if they made the police do what they did."

"Yes, this is possibly true, but most riot training these days specifically instructs trainees to ignore obscenity from the crowds. The Chicago police broke their discipline, but we still don't know whether it was the four-letter words or what preceded or came after them that caused the police to get as rough as they did. My opinion is that the words themselves were not responsible, particularly since the police used them also. One four-letter word will always cancel out another unless it is used in a sentence."

"If these two words go out of fashion because of overuse, what other words will replace them?"

"They've already been replaced. You can get a much more emotional response out of someone by saying 'cops' or 'Vietnam' or 'honky' or 'nigger' than you can get out of 'blank' and 'blank.' "

"People even get mad when you say 'students,' " I said.

"Right. Obscenity can no longer be counted on as a trigger word, and I think this is blanking up the whole English language."

"What can you do about it?"

"Those of us who are interested in the problem are starting a campaign to preserve our four-letter words. We think they should be declared a national heritage and be used as a last resort only in anger and when people can no longer reason together."

MY HOLIDAY WISHES

At every holiday season, my thoughts turn to all Americans, particularly those who spent so many hours of their days and nights watching television and, of course, the commercials.

These are my holiday wishes to all of you:

May you never have iron-poor blood or an Excedrin headache. May your breath always be fresh, so your kid sister won't hand you her mouthwash. May you never perspire in case someone in the family has stolen the underarm deodorant. Grant that your stomach may always be free of demons and that your eight sinus passages will be open and clear.

I pray that your children will never be in the group that has cavities, and if they can't brush after every meal, God grant that you have the wisdom to choose the right toothpaste. I ask that if you have dentures, they never slip out of your mouth, and may you come back to the side that chose the correct hair dressing.

May you never be lacking in breakfast cereal vitamins and may your tresses be so silky and shiny that your husband will have to take you along with him.

May your bra be firm and your girdle comfortable, and may your support stockings make your legs feel elegant and strong.

I pray that your cough will never keep you awake and that your soap will give you twenty-four hour protection. I also wish your facial cream will make you feel young again, and a dove will land on your dishpan hands.

May your shaving cream soften your beard, and may you get more shaves with your blade than with any other comparable brand. May a girl wrestle you to the floor after you use a certain after-shave lotion.

Moreover, may your cigarettes always be mild and contain less tar, and may your beer always be cold and refreshing.

I wish all men clean white shirts, free of ring around the collar, and as for wives, may your piecrusts be flaky and your catsup run slow.

Grant that your refrigerators will always have enough ice and that your oven cleaners will do their job in a jiffy. I pray that moths fear your closets and your mosquitoes drop like flies.

May your sandwiches always be freshly wrapped, and may peanut butter never stick to the roof of your mouth.

I trust the wax will stay on your floor and the stains on your furniture will disappear in seconds.

Furthermore, I wish you a friend at your bank and a loan to tide you over your troubles. And, prithee, if your bank turns you down, may your fingers find a local finance company in the Yellow Pages.

May you have a specially trained insurance agent to help you plan for the future, and if lightning should strike your house, may he be waiting for you with a check at the door.

Grant that your dog gets the right proportion of meat and cereal in his food and that your cat has enough nourishment in the can to keep his coat healthy and clean.

Would that the new car you buy provide speed, comfort, and safety for the whole family and never be recalled to the factory because of a warranty.

I pray that you never get a flat tire on a dark highway and that you never get stuck in the snow because you used the wrong gasoline.

May your sparkplugs spark and your battery never run down. May you win thousands of dollars at gas station sweepstakes, and may you always be able to rent a car with clean ashtrays.

Finally, I wish each and every one of you instant tuning, a clear, ghost-free picture, and on this holiday may all your television tubes be bright.

THE WORK ADDICT

Dr. Nelson Bradley, an Illinois psychiatrist, revealed recently that the United States is being swept by an epidemic of work addiction.

A work addict shows all the characteristics of an alcoholic or narcotics addict. He has a driven craving for work, develops an increasing tolerance for it, and suffers withdrawal symptoms without it, Dr. Bradley said. Like other addictions, this often results in medical and social problems, including bad family relationships with depressed wives and children.

I showed the article to my wife to show her how farfetched psychological theories were getting these days.

"Have you ever heard of anything so ridiculous?" I asked.

She didn't smile. "Will you take the children to the movies this afternoon, so I can get some housework done?"

"I can't. I have to write a piece for the *Ladies' Home Journal*," I said instantly.

"All right. But don't forget we've got to go to the beach next weekend."

"How can I go to the beach when I haven't read *Time* and *Newsweek*?" I said panicking.

"You can read them some other time. You've got to relax once in a while."

"Who says I don't relax? Look how relaxed I am right now?"

"Then why don't you take that typewriter off your knees?" she demanded.

"A little work never hurt anybody," I said. "I only do it to be sociable."

"If you don't want to think of me, why don't you think of the children? How would you like it if someone said your father was a work addict?"

"I'm not a work addict," I cried. "I do a little work in the morning and a little work at night and maybe some in the afternoon. But it's only to soothe my nerves. I could give up work tomorrow and not even miss it."

"Since it's Sunday, why don't you try it?" she suggested.

"All right, I will."

Sunday morning I woke up and grabbed a football.

"Anybody want to play?" I asked at breakfast.

The entire family looked at me suspiciously.

"I'm not kidding," I said. "I feel great. I haven't done a lick of work since I got up. I'm not even going to read the Sunday papers."

We tossed the ball around for a half hour, and suddenly my mouth began to go dry and I started to perspire. I quit the game, shaking, and started for my library. When I got there, I was shocked. My wife had hidden all my typewriting and carbon paper.

I became frenzied. "What did you do with my paper?"

"I locked it up," she said.

"Just give me one sheet," I begged. "I've got to have a sheet."

"No," she said. "I'm doing it for your own good. You'll never lick the habit if I give in to you now."

I went upstairs and tried to take a nap. But every time I closed my eyes, I could see fearsome editors crawling out of the walls with pencils in their sharp teeth.

I woke up screaming, and my wife rushed in.

"One lousy piece of paper," I begged her. "I'll never ask you for anything again."

She took pity on me and unlocked the drawer. "I know I shouldn't do it, but I can't stand you in this state."

I grabbed it and rushed for the typewriter hungrily.

"What are you going to do?"

"Maybe I'll write a story on that crazy psychiatric report I showed you yesterday."

SHAMBLES IN OUR CITIES

Everybody is talking about the problems of the city, but no one seems to be able to do anything about them. The reason nothing can be done about them is that there is an evil, mysterious syndicate at work that has vowed to destroy all cities for human habitation. The organization, known as SHAMBLES, has agents stationed in every key position in municipal government and, through its unbelievable communications system, can bring chaos and destruction to practically any part of a city in a matter of minutes.

I managed to talk to S, the villainous head of SHAM-

BLES, who not only bragged about the great strides SHAMBLES was making, but showed me how the syndicate operates.

I asked S, "Aren't you afraid that if you reveal some of your secrets SHAMBLES will be compromised?"

S chuckled evilly. "Even when they know what we're doing, they can't do a thing to stop us."

He led me into a large room with a lighted street map that covered an entire wall. "Let us suppose," S said, "that traffic is moving smoothly down a street. A spotter immediately flashes word here to SHAMBLES' headquarters, and we dispatch an electrical repair truck with a crew. As soon as the crew arrives on the scene, it starts digging up the road, and in a matter of minutes the street is clogged and traffic has come to a halt. The hole is left in the street until SHAMBLES is assured the traffic will never run smoothly again."

"It doesn't look as if anything is moving at the moment," I said.

S seemed pleased, but suddenly he called to one of the men working at the corner table.

"Is that flow of traffic moving on Park Avenue?"

"Yes, sir. Somebody filled in the hole without our knowledge. We're sending another crew back there to dig a new one."

S took me to the other side of his huge war room and showed me another lighted map.

"You may or may not know it, but SHAMBLES owns a large fleet of trucks. Every morning they are strategically double-parked along busy thoroughfares, so it is impossible for automobiles to get by. This causes people to lose their tempers and start honking their horns, which finally affects the nerves of the people working in the buildings near the streets. The people in the buildings become so unstrung they make mistakes that cost their employers millions of dollars a day."

"How ingenious!" I said.

"We also send agents in old cars, onto highways and bridges, where they break down during the morning and evening rush hours. A skilled agent in an old car can make twenty thousand people late to work—and so irritable that when they get home at night they're ready for divorce."

"And the cost to you is practically nothing," I said.

S led me into another room that looked like a laboratory, with test tubes, microscopes, and lots of highly technical gear.

"This is our air pollution division. If the day is bright and clear and there is no smog in the air, we'll send out trained commando squads to stoke up furnaces and see that chimneys begin belching black smoke. If the wind is blowing in the wrong direction, so the city doesn't get the full benefit of the pollution, we'll order out hundreds of diesel buses to fill the air with obnoxious gases and fumes."

"You think of everything," I said in undisguised admiration.

S said, "We have to, if we want to make any city completely unlivable."

We walked through a corridor and came to a door marked REAL ESTATE. S showed me into a large office with about twenty men at desks manning phones. "The men in this room are in charge of purchasing and wrecking buildings, old as well as new. We'll buy any building and destroy it, so people can't sleep at night or walk safely by it in the daytime."

"Suppose the people won't sell?"

"Then, through our political connections, SHAMBLES will have the property condemned and will build a highway straight through the community. The highways are always built near schools and playgrounds to make them absolutely unsafe for children in the neighborhood."

S took me to another building, but before we went in, he made me stick cotton in my ears. "This is our noise lab," he shouted. "SHAMBLES considers noise one of the most important weapons in its war on cities. It sends out garbage trucks at four o'clock in the morning with specially built garbage grinders on them, just in case the noise of the trucks' motors doesn't wake up the people."

"What are those men down there doing?" I shouted back.

"They're practicing banging the garbage pails against the sides of the truck. Sometimes that can have more effect than the grinder. That control tower over there is connected with the airport. Our agents bring in airplanes for landing in the most populated parts of town, particularly after midnight. We also have firemen and policemen in our pay who sound their sirens all night."

"Are those teen-agers, standing in line over on my left?" I asked.

"Yes. SHAMBLES will pay teen-agers up to ten dollars a day to walk all around the city with transistor radios going full blast."

We left the building and walked over to an open-air area. It looked like a movie set, with attractive shops, a street, and a sidewalk. A gang of men was strewing garbage, newspapers, bottles, and other debris into the street.

S said, "This is where we train the SHAMBLES debris brigades. After a week of training they can go into any street in the city and make a mess of it in less than half an hour."

"What are those men doing with all those dogs?"

"That's our dog division. They're training the dogs to do everything they have to do on the sidewalks instead of near the curbs.

"And over there is a school for abusive taxi drivers. Next to it is a teen-age gang training center, and that building there is where we turn out unfriendly hotel room clerks, snarling waiters, and rude salesgirls for department stores. When they leave here, they'll be able to give any-one in the city a hard time."

"This is really an impressive operation," I told S. "The only question I have left is: Who is behind SHAMBLES?"

S said, "You wouldn't believe me if I told you."

I promised him I would.

He said, "SHAMBLES is a nonprofit foundation sup-ported by people who live in the suburbs to justify their reasons for not living in the city. By making a mess of the cities, they are satisfied the hours they spend every day traveling to and from work are not a waste of time. And while it may cost us a lot of money to keep the syndicate going, it sure makes us feel better when we get home at night."

WHAT'S WRONG WITH PSEUDO-INTELLECTUALS?

As part of his hard-hitting campaign, Vice President Spiro Agnew attacked the pseudo-intellectuals in the United States and blamed them for most of the country's woes.

This caused a great deal of bitterness among America's pseudo-intellectuals, and it's possible that Agnew's strategy has backfired on him.

Mr. Hillary Hazeltine, president of the Pseudo-Intellectual Antidefamation League, held a press conference recently to defend the role of pseudo-intellectuals in the United States and to warn that if Vice President Agnew continued his attacks, he would lose millions of votes in the next election.

"While pseudo-intellectuals do not usually vote as a bloc," Hazeltine said, "they are very sensitive to criticism and certainly would not vote for a man who treats them with so much contempt."

Asked how large the pseudo-intellectual vote was in the United States, Hazeltine replied, "It's hard to say, but we're the ones who subscribe to *Time* magazine, belong to the Book-of-the-Month Club, and watch Leonard Bernstein on television.

"We drive Volkswagens and go to foreign films and buy bullfight posters and, sometimes, drink wine with our meals. Agnew is crazy to mess with us."

"Why would he?"

"He probably doesn't even know what a pseudo-intellectual is. We attend filmed lectures on Tahiti and buy tickets to Edward Albee plays and write letters to the editor of our local newspaper and never miss a PTA meeting and listen to records by Henry Mancini."

Hazeltine continued, "I don't know who Agnew thought he was attacking, but he's stepped on the toes of everyone in this country who quotes David Susskind, who owns a hi-fi stereo record machine, and plays contract bridge on Thursday. We may not watch Ed Sullivan, but we do watch the Smothers brothers and *Laugh-In,* and whenever Marlene Dietrich sings, we buy the house out."

"Then what you're saying, Mr. Hazeltine," a reporter

said, "is that Agnew unknowingly has made fun of the same people that Richard Nixon was appealing to."

"Exactly. We're the forgotten Americans that Nixon is always talking about. We pay our taxes. We work for our money. We don't get involved in crime. The only thing we're trying to do is improve our minds. We might have gone for Nixon if Agnew hadn't given us all that jazz."

"Why do you think he did it?"

"He probably got all mixed up. What he wanted to do was attack the intellectuals, but he was afraid to do it, so he picked on the pseudo-intellectuals instead. If he had attacked the intellectuals in the United States, he might have lost fifty-three votes. But when he went after the pseudo-intellectuals, he took on about ten or fifteen million Americans."

"What does the Pseudo-Intellectual Antidefamation League plan to do about it?"

"We're going to be fair about it and give Agnew a chance to retract what he said about us."

"Do you think he'll do it?"

"Why not? He's retracted practically everything else he's said."

"And if he doesn't?"

"Then we shall notify our membership through the *New Yorker, Atlantic Monthly, Harper's* and *Playboy* that Spiro Agnew is an antipseudo-intellectual, and we will warn them that a vote for Agnew is a vote for Lawrence Welk. We'll let our members take it from there."